CW01084245

FROM BROKEN ATTACHMENTS
TO EARNED SECURITY

The John Bowlby Memorial Conference Monographs Series

FROM BROKEN ATTACHMENTS TO EARNED SECURITY

The Role of Empathy in Therapeutic Change

THE JOHN BOWLBY MEMORIAL CONFERENCE MONOGRAPH 2011

Edited by
Andrew Odgers

The John Bowlby Memorial Conference Monographs
Series Editor: Kate White

KARNAC

First published in 2014 by
Karnac Books Ltd
118 Finchley Road
London NW3 5HT

Copyright © 2014 to Andrew Odgers for the edited collection, and to the individual authors for their contributions.

The rights of the contributors to be identified as the authors of this work have been asserted in accordance with §§ 77 and 78 of the Copyright Design and Patents Act 1988.

All rights reserved. No part of this publication may be reproduced, stored in a retrieval system, or transmitted, in any form or by any means, electronic, mechanical, photocopying, recording, or otherwise, without the prior written permission of the publisher.

British Library Cataloguing in Publication Data

A C.I.P. for this book is available from the British Library

ISBN-13: 978-1-78220-105-2

Typeset by V Publishing Solutions Pvt Ltd., Chennai, India

Printed in Great Britain

www.karnacbooks.com

CONTENTS

ACKNOWLEDGEMENTS

Thanks to the members of the John Bowlby Memorial Conference 2011 planning group: Orit Badouk Epstein, Sarah Benamer, Richard Bowlby, Judy Yellin, and Kate White for their creative work in producing yet another stimulating and ground-breaking conference which has enabled the emergence of this important publication. Also, many thanks to all the contributors to the conference whose profound, creative, and courageous work can now reach a much wider audience.

Particular thanks to our eighteenth John Bowlby Memorial Lecturer 2011, Dr Sandra Bloom, whose outstanding presentation provided a context for the leading edge clinical discussions emerging out of this conference.

A special thank you to Oliver Rathbone for his continuing belief in the value of publishing these monographs and to his colleagues at Karnac Books for their patience and support in their production and publication.

Finally, thank you to Andrew Odgers who has edited this volume with particular skill and attention to detail as well as supporting the contributors to bring into print this amazing set of papers from a remarkable conference.

Kate White,
Series Editor,
John Bowlby Memorial Conference Monographs

ABOUT THE EDITOR AND CONTRIBUTORS

Sandra L. Bloom, M.D. is a psychiatrist, currently Associate Professor of Health Management and Policy and Co-Director of the Center For Nonviolence And Social Justice at the School of Public Health at Drexel University in Philadelphia. From 1980–2001, Dr Bloom directed The Sanctuary programmes, inpatient mental health treatment for adults maltreated as children. Since 2005 she has served as Distinguished Fellow of Andrus Children's Center and has helped to train over 300 programmes nationally and internationally in the Sanctuary Model, a trauma-informed approach to organisational change. Her first book, *Creating Sanctuary: Toward the Evolution of Sane Societies* was just released as a second edition in 2013. The second part of the trilogy of books about the Sanctuary Model. *Destroying Sanctuary: The Crisis in Human Service Delivery Systems* was co-authored with Brian Farragher, the former Chief Operating Officer at Andrus Children's Center and was published in 2010, by Oxford University Press. The third volume of the series, *Restoring Sanctuary: A New Operating System for Trauma-Informed Systems of Care*, was published in 2013 by Oxford University Press. She maintains a website at www.sanctuaryweb.com and the website for the Sanctuary Institute is www.thesanctuaryinstitute.org.

Sue Gerhardt is a practising psychotherapist in private practice. Since the late 1990s, she has played a significant role in drawing attention to the importance of early intervention in infancy. Inspired by the work of Daniel Stern, she co-founded the Oxford Parent Infant Project (OXPIP), a charity providing parent/infant psychotherapy for parents and babies, which today helps around fifty families a week in Oxfordshire. In 2004, she published *Why Love Matters: How Affection Shapes a Baby's Brain*, bringing the pioneering work of Allan Schore and the latest scientific findings in neurobiology to a wider audience. Most recently, she has argued in *The Selfish Society*, (2010) that infancy is not just of concern to parents but has a central place in our culture and in transmitting social values. Sue has two grown-up children and lives in Oxford.

Jane Haynes trained as a Jungian psychoanalyst after a Freudian analysis. Still indebted to this past, she now regards herself as a psychotherapist—whose primary tool to understanding the trickster energies of the psyche is not primarily through interpretation but through a dialogic relationship—in which attachment theory has a pivotal role. She wrote and was then forced to self publish—having been rejected by every publisher—*Who Is It That Can Tell Me Who I Am?* Which, after it was shortlisted for the PEN literary autobiography prize, was re-published by Constable. She is the editor of several books including, *When a Princess Dies, a Jungian collection of papers on the death of Princess Diana*.

She has just finished writing her latest book with Dr Martin Scurr, *Doctors,* which is a study of what goes on inside of the doctor's mind when he drops his 'mask'. Publisher to be announced.

Oliver James is a chartered clinical psychologist and registered as a psychotherapist at The Bowlby Centre. He studied social anthropology at Cambridge University and trained as a child clinical psychologist at Nottingham University, and worked as a research fellow at Brunel University and then as a clinical psychologist in the Cassel Mental Hospital for six years, before becoming an author, journalist (he has had columns in six national newspapers), TV producer, radio broadcaster, and television presenter. He is the author of the bestsellers *They F*** You Up—How to Survive Family Life* (2002) and *Affluenza—How to be Successful and Stay Sane* (2007). He has also written *How Not To F*** Them Up*

(2010), *The Selfish Capitalist*, (2008), *Contented Dementia* (2008), *Britain on the Couch—How Keeping Up With The Joneses Had Depressed Us Since 1950* (1997), and *Juvenile Violence in a Winner-Loser Culture* (1995). He has contributed articles to scientific journals in recent years, including the *Journal of Epidemiology and Community Health* and *The Psychologist*. He has acted as an adviser to both New Labour and the Conservative Party.

Andrew Odgers studied psychology at university in South Africa, and trained as a psychotherapist when he moved to London over twenty years ago. He is a UKCP registered attachment-based psychoanalytic psychotherapist, having trained at the Institute for Self Analysis which grew into The Bowlby Centre of today. He has taught and facilitated professional development seminars at The Bowlby Centre. Andrew now works as a management consultant and focuses on leadership development, working with management teams, exploring their development issues and team dynamics. He is also an executive coach. Andrew co-chaired the conference.

Anastasia Patrikiou is a psychoanalytic psychotherapist. After training and working as an architect for a number of years, she completed a post-graduate diploma in counselling at Strathclyde University and an attachment-based psychoanalytic psychotherapy training at The Bowlby Centre. She has been in private practice since 2003, and is currently also working with people with eating difficulties at the Priory Hospital. She worked in NHS primary care for a number of years and developed and managed a pilot counselling service in the voluntary sector to make therapy accessible to marginalised groups for a charity. This was successfully mainstreamed. Originating from a migratory background, she has a particular interest in trauma, loss, and the impact of displacement on relational structures and identity narratives.

Eleanor Richards was a lecturer and researcher in musicology and worked in community arts before training in music therapy in the early 1990s and subsequently in psychotherapy at The Bowlby Centre. She is now a psychotherapist and supervisor in private practice. Until 2013 she worked in the Cambridgeshire and Peterborough NHS Foundation Trust, with a special interest in working with people with learning disabilities. She is also a senior lecturer and supervisor on the

MA in music therapy at Anglia Ruskin University, Cambridge. She is joint author/editor of *Music Therapy and Groupwork: Sound Company* (2002) and of *Supervision of Music Therapy* (2008). In her continuing musical life she is active as a player and improviser.

Kate White is a training therapist, supervisor, teacher and formerly chair of the clinical training committee at The Bowlby Centre. She is also editor of the journal, *Attachment: New Directions in Psychotherapy and Relational Psychoanalysis* and series editor of The *John Bowlby Memorial Conference Monographs*. Prior to training as a psychotherapist Kate was a senior lecturer at the South Bank University, London, in the department of nursing and community health studies. She has used her extensive experience in adult education to contribute to the innovative psychotherapy curriculum developed at The Bowlby Centre. In addition to working as an individual psychotherapist, Kate writes about psychotherapy education and runs workshops on the themes of attachment and trauma in clinical practice. Informed by her experience of growing up in South Africa, she has long been interested in the impact of race and culture on theory and on clinical practice. She has edited two books, *Unmasking Race, Culture and Attachment in the Psychoanalytic Space; What do we see? What do we think? What do we feel?* (Karnac, 2006) and *Touch: Attachment and the Body.* (Karnac, 2004) and co-edited a three others, one with Joseph Schwartz, *Sexuality and Attachment in Clinical Practice*, (Karnac, 2007), a second with Sarah Benamer, *Trauma and Attachment* (Karnac, 2008), and a third with Judy Yellin, *Shattered States, Disorganised Attachment and its Repair*, (Karnac, 2012).

INTRODUCTION

The eighteenth Bowlby memorial conference was held in London in March 2011. Sir Richard Bowlby opened the conference, and this monograph reproduces the excellent papers that were presented.

We began with the known—that painful insecure attachments, emerging from relational trauma, result in difficulties in empathy and attunement whether between parent and child, within adult relationships, between client and therapist, and in organisational contexts. The challenge is how to re-establish a secure sense of self, mutuality, and the capacity for inter/intra-subjectivity with all these relationships?

The conference focused on what was required within all these settings in order to facilitate empathy and attunement and ultimately the achievement of earned security. Our six speakers explored how the dynamics of insecure attachment manifest themselves both at the micro-level of one-to-one relationships, and also at the macro-level of groups and organisations and the wider society within which they are embedded.

Our understanding of the parent infant relationship, and the essential role of empathy in the development of children's growing capacity to recognise and respond to the subjective experience of others, has greatly increased in the light of research into attachment and its neurobiology.

We know a good deal about how emotional development can go awry, and how parents' and carers' own attachment histories can impact, for good or ill, on a child's sense of self. But how does this knowledge and understanding of what can go wrong translate into clinical practice? What skills do we need and how do we need to be using them in the consulting room in order to help clients move from an insecure attachment state of mind to "earned security"?

Our speakers also addressed questions such as: what about our wider society? Can we apply what we have learned about security of attachment and relationships between individuals to this wider context? Can we identify the dynamics of trauma and insecure attachment within groups and organisations, particularly organisations which engage in providing health and therapeutic services? What are the additional stresses on such organisations in a climate of austerity and cuts and how do they impact upon our ability as therapists to offer a secure base of support not only to our clients in therapy, but also to each other as colleagues and co-workers within our professional organisations and in our wider professional communities?

Our speakers each presented challenging and exciting papers, approaching their topics with extreme sensitivity, sharing intimate details about their own work, including their doubts and challenges, to provide us with a rich picture of working one-to-one and within organisations to effect recovery. Their willingness to take the risks of sharing their work and describe the challenges of true empathic relations generated lively discussion during the event and beyond.

A substantial amount of reworking of each conference paper was undertaken by the authors in preparation for this publication to ensure that the latest research was quoted and to protect their clients and ensure that confidentiality was maintained.

Sue Gerhardt in her paper, "The effort of empathy" describes what we have learned about empathy, and how it has been used in psychoanalysis and psychotherapy more widely. She outlines how our own experience of being parented can develop or actually inhibit our ability to empathise with others. She shares how hard it is to develop true empathy, using her own work with two clients to convey the challenge and the effort required. She provides astute observations of the impact of her approach on her clients and the therapy relationship.

Oliver James' paper is entitled "Love bombing: a simple self-help intervention for parents to reset their child's emotional thermostat".

He provides a challenging critique of our society and its impact on child rearing. He gives a detailed summary of the research on the impact of lack of maternal responsiveness, and the consistency and type of early care on the later development of the child. He acknowledges the pressures on parents in a modern age and how their own experience of being parented affected them, but challenges the view that children's behaviour becomes fixed and is largely determined by genes. He gives a lively account of his discovery of a method he has called "love bombing", an intensive, brief (ideally forty eight hour) time for a parent and child, offering the child unlimited love and control. The results from more than one hundred families are astounding.

Jane Haynes, in a unique collaboration with her client, Harry Whitehead, presented a paper entitled: "To shed what still attempts to cling as if attached by thorns" (R.M Rilke). Jane questions whether a truly empathic attitude is possible in therapy. She describes her experience of being Harry's therapist, the highs and lows, and her doubts at some of his accounts and achievements. Harry then gives his account of his therapy from his own perspective. This provides an astonishing and deeply moving dual perspective of an intensive, relational therapeutic process.

Sandra Bloom, delivered the John Bowlby memorial lecture. Her presentation ranged between the intra-personal to the societal, exploring what happens when people who have a history of exposure to adversity, toxic stress, and trauma and have complex problems are treated in health and human service delivery environments. She eloquently describes how these caregiving organisations are living, complex, adaptive systems, and that, like individuals, they can be traumatised. The results of this traumatic experience can be as devastating for organisations as it is for individuals, and destructive processes can then occur within and between organisations which mirror or "parallel" the processes for which clients seek help. She eloquently describes the profound effect this has and in particular discusses the loss of empathy at every level. She then sets out the necessary, conscious process of creating Sanctuary—a deliberate shift of approach for all staff and clients—aimed at changing the culture of these organisations and creating a community.

Finally Eleanor Richards and Anastasia Patrikiou each provide us with a detailed case study from their own practices.

Eleanor's paper entitled "What happens after this quiet bit? I may have to leave now." describes her work with a client for whom music is the way to feel alive. She describes the painstaking process of reaching out to someone who is bright and articulate but affectively disengaged. Her own musical background and rhythms give a lyrical feel to this very moving and profound presentation.

Anastasia in "Empathy and earned security: reciprocal influences, ruptures and shifts in the psychotherapeutic process" looks at how the presence or absence of empathy in the therapist impacts the therapeutic dyad. She provides an excellent historical overview of the roots of empathy, defining and describing the concept of empathy and its development in the psychotherapeutic world. Her clinical illustration depicts how closely a client will monitor a therapist to see if they are really understanding and connecting empathically with their experience.

These six papers make a significant contribution to the field of attachment and our understanding of how child rearing affects each aspect of our lives, from the interpersonal to the organisational and societal. Each paper moves beyond the academic and theoretical to provide answers to the many difficult questions we raised at the beginning of the conference.

The practical, sometimes step by step explanations of the use of empathy in one-to-one clinical work, in health service organisations or society generally, offer a positive and hopeful way forward. All of the presenters faced up to the challenges of repairing or reversing the impact of derailed attachments and the toxic impact of trauma, offering a realistic but hopeful route to improved relating and healthier attachments.

We believe that this publication will be a valuable resource for students, seasoned practitioners, and health service professionals alike who want to enhance their understanding of empathy and attachment in this demanding field.

CHAPTER ONE

Attachment theory and the John Bowlby Memorial Lecture 2011: a short history*

Kate White

This year we mark the eighteenth anniversary of the first John Bowlby memorial lecture given by Colin Murray Parkes on the theme of mourning and loss, which was a fitting recognition of Bowlby's great contribution to the understanding of human grief and sadness, and his clinical observations of separation and loss that laid down the foundations of attachment theory. This year's lecturer, Sandy Bloom was a presenter at that first conference and it is an honour that she returns to deliver the John Bowlby memorial lecture 2011 on the theme of "Creating, destroying, and restoring Sanctuary within caregiving organisations", which takes the application of attachment theory into the important and complex arena of organisational life.

In the years which have followed that first conference, attachment theory, in the words of Cassidy and Shaver (2008, xi), has produced "one of the broadest, most profound and most creative lines of research in twentieth century (and now twenty-first century) psychology". Nevertheless, given the hostility of the psychoanalytic establishment to Bowlby's ideas, it has only been in the last two decades,

---

*Based on an original article by Bernice Laschinger.

during which there have been dramatic advances in the congruent disciplines of infancy research and relational psychoanalysis, that the clinical relevance of attachment theory has been unquestionably established.

Indeed, it has been the development of its clinical applications, in tandem with its evolving convergence with psychoanalysis and trauma theory, that has been central to our practice at The Bowlby Centre. Looking back, our very early links with Bowlby's work were forged by one of our founders, John Southgate, who had undergone clinical supervision with John Bowlby himself. Bowlby's understanding of the nature of human relatedness became primary in our theoretical framework and practice. It contributed directly to our emergence as an attachment-based psychoanalytic centre in 1992.

In 2007 the John Bowlby memorial conference marked the centenary of John Bowlby's birth in 1907. One of the outstanding psychoanalysts of the twentieth century, as a theory builder and reformer, his societal impact and influence on social policy have been greater than that of any other. He has been described by Diana Diamond as "the Dickens of psychoanalytic theory": he illuminated the human experiences of attachment and loss as vividly as Dickens represented those of poverty and deprivation.

The origins of Bowlby's ideas lay in his early work with children displaced through war or institutionalisation. This led him to the conviction that at the heart of traumatic experience lay parental loss and prolonged separation from one's parents. His landmark report for the World Health Organization, *Maternal Care and Mental Health*, enabled him to establish definitively the primary link between environmental trauma and the disturbed development of children (1952).

With these understandings, he entered the public arena to bring about change in the way childhood suffering was addressed by the adult world. Bowlby's work created a bridge over the chasm between individual and social experience and hence between the personal and the political.

There is congruence between the social and therapeutic perspectives of John Bowlby and those of the John Bowlby memorial lecturer in 2008, Judith Herman, author of *Father Daughter Incest* (2000) and *Trauma and Recovery* (1992). She, too, has directed her life's work to the "restoring of connections" between the private and public worlds in which traumatic experience takes place; but her focus has been on the traumatic experiences that take place in adulthood. She has shown the parallels between private terrors such as rape and domestic violence, and public traumas such as political terrorism. Her conceptual framework for psychotherapy with traumatised people points to the major importance of attachment in the empowerment of the survivor. She writes: "Recovery can take place only within the context of relationships; it cannot occur in isolation" (1992, p. 133).

Bowlby had also sought to bridge the chasm between clinician and researcher. His preparedness to leave the closed world of the psychoanalysis of his time in order to make links with other disciplines, such as animal studies and academic psychology, was vital in the building up of attachment theory. The documented and filmed sequence of children's responses to separation in terms of protest, detachment, and despair, as researched by James Robertson, provided evidence of separation anxiety. The impact of these ideas on the development of the care of children in hospital has been enormous. The 2001 John Bowlby memorial lecturer, Michael Rutter, discussed institutional care and the role of the state in promoting recovery from neglect and abuse. His lecture was a testament to the continuing relevance of Bowlby's thinking to contemporary social issues.

Although Bowlby joined the British Psychoanalytical Society in the 1930s and received his training from Joan Riviere and Melanie Klein, he became increasingly sceptical of their focus on the inner fantasy life of the child rather than real life experience, and tended towards what would now be termed a relational approach. Thus, in searching for a theory which could explain the anger and distress of separated young children, Bowlby turned to disciplines outside psychoanalysis such as ethology. He became convinced of the relevance of animal and particularly primate behaviour to our understanding of the normal process of attachment. These relational concepts presented a serious challenge to the closed world of psychoanalysis in the 1940s, and earned Bowlby the hostility of his erstwhile colleagues for several decades.

The maintenance of physical proximity by a young animal to a preferred adult is found in a number of animal species. This suggested to Bowlby that attachment behaviour has a survival value, the most likely function of which is that of care and protection, particularly from predators. It is activated by conditions such as sickness, fear, and fatigue. The threat of loss leads to anxiety and anger; actual loss leads to anger and sorrow. When efforts to restore the bond fail, attachment behaviour may diminish, but will persist at an unconscious level and may become reactivated by reminders of the lost adult, or new experiences of loss.

Attachment theory's basic premise is that, from the beginning of life, the baby human has a primary need to establish an emotional bond with a caregiving adult. Attachment is seen as a source of human motivation as fundamental as those of food and sex. Bowlby (1979) postulated that:

> Attachment behaviour is any form of behaviour that results in a person attaining or maintaining proximity to some other preferred and differentiated individual [...]. While especially evident during early childhood, attachment behaviour is held to characterise human beings from the cradle to the grave. (p. 129)

Attachment theory highlights the importance of mourning in relation to trauma and loss. An understanding of the relevance of this to therapeutic practice was a vital element in the foundation of The Bowlby Centre. The consequences of disturbed and unresolved mourning processes was a theme taken up by Colin Murray Parkes when he gave the first John Bowlby memorial lecture in 1993.

Mary Ainsworth, an American psychologist who became Bowlby's lifelong collaborator, established the interconnectedness between attachment behaviour, caregiving in the adult, and exploration in the child. While the child's need to explore, and the need for proximity might seem contradictory, they are in fact complementary. It is the mother's provision of a secure base, to which the child can return after exploration, which enables the development of self-reliance and autonomy. Ainsworth developed the "strange situation test" for studying individual differences in the attachment patterns of young children. She was able to correlate these to their mother's availability and responsiveness. Her work provided both attachment theory and psychoanalysis with empirical support for some basic premises. This provided the necessary link between attachment concepts and their application to individual experience in a clinical setting.

Over the last two decades the perspective of attachment theory has been greatly extended by the work of Mary Main who was another John Bowlby memorial lecturer. She developed the "adult attachment interview" in order to study the unconscious processes which underlie the behavioural pattern of attachment identified by Mary Ainsworth.

Further support came from the perspective of infant observation and developmental psychology developed by yet another John Bowlby memorial lecturer, Daniel Stern. The John Bowlby memorial lecturer for 2000, Allan Schore, presented important developments in the new field of neuro-psychoanalysis, describing emerging theories of how attachment experiences in early life shape the developing brain.

The links between attachment theory and psychoanalysis have also been developed. Jo Klein, a great supporter of The Bowlby Centre and also a former contributor to the John Bowlby memorial conference, has explored these links in psychotherapeutic practice. In particular, the 1998 Bowlby lecturer, the late Stephen Mitchell, identified a paradigm shift away from drive theory within psychoanalysis. His proposed that the "relational matrix" links attachment theory to other relational psychoanalytic theories which find so much resonance in the current social and cultural climate. Within this area of convergence, between attachment research and developmental psychoanalysis, the 1999 John Bowlby memorial lecturer, Peter Fonagy, has developed the concept of "mentalization", extending our understanding of the importance of the reflective function, particularly in adversity.

In a similar vein, the work of Beatrice Beebe, the 2001 John Bowlby memorial lecturer, represents another highly creative development in the unfolding relational narrative of the researcher-clinician dialogue. Her unique research has demonstrated how the parent–infant interaction creates a distinct system organised by mutual influence and regulation which are reproduced in the adult therapeutic relationship.

In the movement to bring the body into the forefront of relational theory and practice, the 2003 John Bowlby memorial lecturer, Susie Orbach, has been a leading pioneer. It was the publication of her groundbreaking books, *Fat is a Feminist Issue* (1978) and *Hunger Strike* (1986) which introduced a powerful and influential approach to the study of the body in its social context. Over the last decade, one of her major interests has been the construction of sexuality and bodily experience in the therapeutic relationship.

The 2004 John Bowlby memorial lecturer, Jody Messler Davies, has made major contributions to the development of the relational model. Her integration of trauma theory and relational psychoanalysis led to new understandings of transference-countertransference as a vehicle for expressing traumatic experience (Davies & Frawley, 1994).

Kimberlyn Leary, our John Bowlby memorial lecturer in 2005, illuminated the impact of racism on the clinical process. The importance of her contribution lay in her understanding of the transformative potential inherent in the collision of two "racialised subjectivities" in the therapeutic process. She showed the possibility for reparation when both therapist and client break the silence surrounding their difference.

The contribution of the 2006 John Bowlby memorial lecturer, Bessel van der Kolk, to the understanding of post-traumatic stress as a developmental trauma disorder has been seminal, (2005). His book, *Psychological Trauma*, was the first to consider the impact of trauma on the entire person, integrating neurobiological, interpersonal, and social perspectives (1987).

Within this tradition of great trauma theorists, the contribution of John Bowlby memorial lecturer, 2007, Judith Herman, a collaborator of Bessel van der Kolk, has been outstanding. As a teacher, researcher, and clinician, her life's work has been directed to survivors of trauma. Her landmark book, *Trauma and Recovery* (1992) is considered to have changed the way we think about trauma. Bridging the world of war veterans, prisoners of war, and survivors of domestic and sexual abuse, she has shown that psychological trauma can only be understood in a social context.

In 2008 our John Bowlby memorial lecturer was Arietta Slade, a widely published clinician, researcher, and teacher. Her work has been enormously significant in the movement to link attachment theory with clinical ideas (1999b, 2008). She has pioneered attachment-based approaches to clinical work with both adults and children, including the development of parental reflective functioning and the relational contexts of play and early symbolisation. There is also congruence between her current work and the spirit of Bowlby's early clinical observations. She has shifted the therapeutic focus away from the formal categorisation of attachment patterns, to questions about how the attachment system functions to regulate fear and distress within the therapeutic process, significantly where there are "dynamic disruptions".

Arietta Slade's work represents a highly significant development in the application of attachment theory to clinical work (1999a). Following on the work of Main (1994) and Fonagy (1999), she has demonstrated how an attachment-based understanding of the development of representation and affect regulation in the child and his or her mother offers us potentially transformative insights into the nature of the therapeutic process and change.

In 2009 we were honoured to welcome Amanda Jones to give the John Bowlby memorial lecture. She presented the work she had carried out with troubled parents and their children—highlighted in the television series *Help Me Love My Baby*. Her work has been acclaimed for its capacity to demonstrate the effectiveness of interventions where the parent is offered a long term compassionate attachment relationship in which their own story of trauma is shared. This provides a possibility for reflectiveness and intergenerational change.

Our John Bowlby memorial lecturer in 2010 was Jude Cassidy, a pioneer in the attachment tradition of research with clinical applications. She was a student of Bowlby's primary collaborator Mary Ainsworth and has extended attachment theory's reach in both the fields of childhood and adolescence. As an author and editor she has had a prominent role in the publication of attachment theory, research findings, and their clinical application. Jude Cassidy is professor of psychology at the University of Maryland and director of the Maryland Child and Family Development Laboratory. She received her Ph.D. in 1986 from the University of Virginia where her mentor was Mary Ainsworth. Jude Cassidy's research includes a focus on early intervention. Her concerns are wide ranging focusing on attachment, social and emotional development in children and adolescents, social information-processing, peer relations, and longitudinal prediction of adolescent risk behaviour. These were all areas that were pertinent to our theme in 2009 of "Attachment in the twenty-first century; where next?"

This year's John Bowlby memorial lecturer is Dr Sandra L. Bloom, who has a long association with The Bowlby Centre as she has been our consultant on trauma for many years. Sandy Bloom is a psychiatrist, currently associate professor of health management and policy and co-director of the Center for Nonviolence and Social Justice at the school of public health at Drexel University in Philadelphia.

She is best known to us through her imaginative and pioneering work for twenty-one years as director of the Sanctuary programmes, an inpatient mental health intervention for adults maltreated as children. Here she developed a humane and compassionate centre caring for those traumatised in early life using the work of John Bowlby as its central conceptual framework.

Since 2005 she has served as Distinguished Fellow of Andrus Children's Center and has helped to train over a hundred programmes nationally and internationally in the Sanctuary model, an attachment based and trauma-informed approach to organisational change. This work was first written about in 1997 and is now published in a second edition, *Creating Sanctuary: Toward the Evolution of Sane Societies* (Bloom, 2013). A more recent book, co-authored with Brian Farragher, *Destroying Sanctuary: The Crisis in Human Service Delivery*, was published by Oxford University Press in 2010, and the third volume of the series, *Restoring Sanctuary*, is out now, (Bloom & Farragher, 2013). She maintains a website at www.sanctuaryweb.com where much of her innovative work can be found.

References

Bloom, S. L. (2013). *Creating Sanctuary: Toward the Evolution of Sane Societies*, (2nd edition). New York: Routledge.

Bloom, S. L., & Farragher, B. (2010). *Destroying Sanctuary: The Crisis in Human Service Delivery Systems*. New York: Oxford University Press.

Bloom, S. L., & Farragher, B. (2013). *Restoring Sanctuary: A New Operating System for Trauma-Informed Systems of Care*. New York: Oxford University Press.

Bowlby, J. (1952). *Maternal Care and Mental Health*, (2nd edition). World Health Organization: Monograph Series, No. 2. Geneva, Switzerland: World Health Organization.

Bowlby, J. (1979). *The Making and Breaking of Affectional Bonds*. London: Tavistock.

Cassidy, J., & Shaver, P. (2008). *Handbook of Attachment: Theory, Research and Clinical Applications*. New York: Guilford Press.

Davies, J. M., & Frawley, M. G. (1994). *Treating the Adult Survivor of Childhood Sexual Abuse: A Psychoanalytic Perspective*. New York: Basic.

Fonagy, P. (1999). Psychoanalytic theory from the point of view of attachment theory and research. In: J. Cassidy & P. R. Shaver (Eds.), *Handbook of Attachment Theory and Research*. New York: Guilford Press.

Herman, J. L. (1992). *Trauma and Recovery: The Aftermath of Violence from Domestic Abuse to Political Terror*. New York: Basic.

Herman, J. L. (2000). *Father Daughter Incest*. Cambridge, MA: Harvard University Press.

Main, M. (1994). A move to the level of representation in the study of attachment organization: Implications for psychoanalysis. *Bulletin of the British Psycho-Analytical Society*: 1–15.

Orbach, S. (1978). *Fat is a Feminist Issue*. London: Paddington Press.

Orbach, S. (1986). *Hunger Strike, The Anorectic's Struggle as a Metaphor for Our Time*. London: Faber and Faber.

Slade, A. (1999a). Representation, symbolization and affect regulation. *Psychoanalytic Inquiry, 19*: 797–830.

Slade, A. (1999b). Attachment theory and research. In: *Handbook of Attachment: Theory, Research and Clinical Applications* (pp. 575–591). New York: Guilford Press.

Slade, A. (2008). The move from categories to process: Attachment phenomena and clinical evaluation in attachment. *New Directions in Psychotherapy and Relational Psychoanalysis, 2(1)*: 89–105.

van der Kolk, B. (1987). *Psychological Trauma*. Washington, D.C.: American Psychiatric Press.

van der Kolk, B. (2005). Developmental trauma disorder. *Psychiatric Annals, 35(5)*: 401–408.

CHAPTER TWO

The effort of empathy

Sue Gerhardt

Ababy cries persistently and looks away from his mother. The mother makes soothing noises and seems to be doing all the "right" things, yet there is a quality of detachment about her responses; she looks embarrassed and awkward. Her face is fixed in a half smile. She isn't able to soothe her baby. Why is that? This is a mother who has spent very little time with her baby and isn't very comfortable with him. She is afraid of failing as a mother. As a child she didn't receive empathic parenting herself, and never really wanted to become a mother. She is certainly *trying* to do the right thing and trying to understand him: she comes up with various interpretations of her baby's behaviour, deciding at first that he must be hungry (yet he rejects the bottle she offers) and then concluding "he's angry". Despite these attempts to make sense of his behaviour, she doesn't convey a willingness to enter into his experience or to *feel with* her baby.

Many people think of empathy as something to do with some sort of cosy ideal of mothering, and perfect attunement, and being nice. Some people have argued that therapy based on empathy is a kind of "safe analysis" where there are no ethical dilemmas, no sexuality, no challenges. The analytic therapist Andrew Samuels is one such, who calls it, rather evocatively, "a 'milky' worldview" (Samuels, 1996, p. 301).

11

But is empathy so easy and safe? Not for this mother.

This mother is struggling to live up to an idealised mother image. She is trying her best to be "nice" and to get her baby to be "nice" to her. She does her best to get the baby to smile at her and wants to deflect what she experiences as his "anger". But such efforts are actually a barrier to empathy. Implicitly, they reflect the view that human relations are fragile and have to be kept "nice" by defensive means. This mother finds her own difficult feelings very hard to bear. Her discomfort with negative emotion means that her baby's negative arousal is so aversive, that she needs to keep him at arm's length. She cannot really get into the baby's feelings with him, and help the baby to regulate them. Instead, she gives the impression that she wants the baby's feelings to go away.

Clearly, even in this most basic and primal human relation between mother and baby, empathy is not that easy.

How to develop empathy

Let me be more precise in defining what I mean by empathy. The most basic level of empathy is probably fairly effortless. It has been called "emotional contagion"—that bodily resonance we have with other people's feelings which is probably generated in part by our mirror neurons (these respond to other people's body language by activating the areas of our own brains which generate similar behaviours, giving us a rough and ready sense of how others feel).

The next level of empathy is affect attunement, as described by Daniel Stern (1985). This is also fairly automatic and unconscious. It *builds* on our ability to resonate to others states, but adds an extra element—of non-verbal communication. When someone is attuned, they instinctively let the other person know that they've understood how they feel, by responding in another sensory modality. For example, if a client comes in with a slow, heavy way of moving that conveys sadness, my voice might automatically adjust to a gentle, low tone. This lets the client know that I have empathically recognised her inner state. If I simply imitated her heavy movements, she would know that I had noticed her *external* behaviour—but she wouldn't necessarily feel that I had understood the sadness (and of course, if I said a cheerful and loud "hello", she'd probably experience me as quite unattuned—perhaps in the same way that the baby might have felt, seeing his mother smiling anxiously at him when he was crying).

Although for the most part attunement happens unconsciously, I think one can also deliberately "tune in" and sensitise oneself to the other person's bodily signals—something Freud (1912b, pp. 115–116) described as turning your own unconscious receptively towards the "transmitting unconscious of the patient". We can also consciously choose to give verbal feedback about the way we perceive someone's feelings, to let them know that we have understood how they feel.

Empathy proper is at the top of this pyramid and is a complex higher brain achievement. It is a process which is *rooted* in the lower levels of bodily resonance and attunement, but it introduces a more cognitive element. When you empathise, you consciously draw on your own self awareness. You think back to your own past emotional experiences, to help you imagine what someone else is feeling. While this is happening, you also normally suspend your own goals, and give priority to *feeling with* the other person, whilst still remaining aware of your own feelings—which might be very different. All of this complex behaviour activates the higher emotional brain areas, particularly the medial pre-frontal cortex (Decety, 2011).

It takes time and effort for this ability to develop, and it depends on having built up a memory bank of encounters with other people, and being able to recognise and identify those emotional experiences.

Babies don't yet have a full repertoire of social experience. To build up their self-awareness, they need consistent help from empathic parental figures to identify their emotions, to make them conscious, and to name them. This starts very young indeed and depends on having parents who recognise their baby as an intentional being and can accurately "read" their baby's states (as the mother I discussed earlier could not). It takes about eighteen months of parental feedback just to get to the point when a child has enough self-awareness to be able to recognise himself as a person in the mirror. This is how long it takes to build up enough connections in a child's orbitofrontal cortex to achieve a sort of mental overview of his basic emotions, such as anger and fear—and the ability to use this awareness to achieve some control (a "pause button") over his gut responses. Until an individual has achieved these developmental tasks for himself, it is hard for him to recognise how other people's behaviour is also motivated by emotions and the struggle to manage and control them.

These are the capacities that are then elaborated for the rest of our lives. We build on our basic understanding of emotions to develop a more nuanced appreciation of the variety of human feelings. We build on those beginnings of self-control to develop more mature ethical capacities like putting other people's needs ahead of our own. We build on the basic memory bank of self experiences to create a whole complex narrative of our personal experiences over time.

Effects of unempathic care

If you have not experienced empathy from your early caregivers it is more difficult to respond to others with empathy. It is hard to muster it up from a weakly connected medial prefrontal cortex. What comes more naturally is to react to the other person without thinking, and without awareness of their feelings. This kind of reactive behaviour is familiar to me from my own childhood. Although the parent figures in my early life could be affectionate, they were not interested in thinking about other people's feelings and regarded emotions as a "weakness". As a result, they were often impulsively critical and aggressive. At some unconscious level, I was drawn to psychotherapy to find a way to overcome the deficits such a childhood had left me with. I remember when I first started practising as a psychotherapist, I found it as exhausting as going to the gym to strengthen new muscles. I certainly didn't feel it was easy; in fact it was a tremendous effort to take the perspective of my clients and to *feel with* them.

My childhood experiences were by no means unique. For most of the twentieth century, many parent/child relationships were relatively harsh and coercive. Historically, the predominant form of parenting has been a harsh one, rooted in the idea of original sin (as I explored in *The Selfish Society* (Gerhardt, 2010)). In this world view, babies are seen as self–centred and manipulative and the parent's duty is to teach the child how to behave and to know his place in a hierarchical society. Early psychoanalysts, who very often had been on the receiving end of such parenting themselves, often shared these cultural beliefs which played a part in psychoanalytical theories such as those of innate aggression and destructiveness.

Empathy was not regarded as essential to psychoanalysis. As Josephine Klein once pointed out, identifying with others has often been regarded as unsuitable behaviour for professionals. It might "weaken their ability to 'deal with' the client" (Klein, 1995, p. 13). At times, this tendency can extend into hostility. There were times when I was doing my psychotherapy training in the 1990s, when I was shocked to hear analysts speak about their patients using the same contemptuous tone I had heard so often in my family. They regularly referred to their clients as "babies" who needed to grow up or "victims" who needed to take responsibility for themselves. As Jean Knox has pointed out, this language matters, because the model of the mind you use "is closely coupled to and prescriptive of specific clinical techniques" (Knox, 2011, p. 188).

The negative transference became the centrepiece of this combative clinical approach. Some analysts assumed a position of power and acted in many ways like punitive parents who were trying to make the patient take responsibility for her "bad" feelings. When, as a trainee, I took some work I was doing with a sexually abused young woman to supervision, the advice I got from the supervisor was to: "*destroy* her masochism, make her see her murderous feelings, force her to see how she wants to control others". Of course, the client did need help in identifying and expressing her ambivalence and rage towards her parents (or even me)—but not, in my view, by deliberately arousing or intensifying her fear and anger in the transference.

Fortunately psychoanalytic psychotherapy—and parenting—have both moved in the direction of a more empathic stance. In the later twentieth century, Winnicott, Fairbairn, and Kohut, changed psychoanalytic thinking. Person-centred therapies also spread. More recently, relational psychoanalysis has taken off. Most important of all, the rapid growth of research based on Bowlby's attachment thinking confirmed the impact of actual relational experiences, particularly in infancy—an understanding which has been given a tremendous boost in the last few decades by the scientific work done in developmental psychology, and neurobiology.

All this research has given us a clear picture of how new attachment relationships, whether between parent and baby, or therapist and client, are formed. The relationship is a regulatory one. It involves the creation of a safe base, which comes about through sensitivity—tuning in and noticing feelings—and responsiveness—turn-taking and mutual feedback—as well as repairing any misunderstandings or failures to respond. These are the processes we know are at the heart of effective attachment relationships, processes which generate confidence that the attachment figure will be available to help regulate emotions when needed—particularly at times of distress (Schore & Schore, 2008).

The emphasis on emotional regulation has given new impetus to treatments such as mindfulness based therapies and energy techniques. It is certainly at the heart of my work with parents and babies, and has helped me clarify what I am doing in all my clinical work.

Kirstie and Millie: physiological regulation vs. empathy

I now want to turn to a discussion of some clinical examples, to show the relevance of empathy in the developmental process. Kirstie and Millie were another mother and baby who were just getting to know each other when they first came to see me. Kirstie had recently arrived from Scotland and had no support system in England. She was a very young parent who was referred to me through a professional agency when she was pregnant with Millie, with the brief to monitor her relationship with her new baby because of serious neglect of her older child.

At first, I wondered whether the agency was being over-cautious. Kirstie was devoted to her new baby when Millie was born, breast-feeding her, carrying her everywhere in a sling, sleeping with her in bed at night. It seemed to me that this physical closeness and constant proximity would be highly beneficial for Millie. I expected it to enable Kirstie to respond to Millie's signals quickly and to protect her from stress, facilitating an effective soothing system, as well as a balanced stress response, leading to Millie being able to establish her own self-regulation.

Yet, when I observed Kirstie and Millie together, when Millie was about three months old, I began to notice some less positive features of their interaction. Although Kirstie was tuned in to Millie's bodily needs for milk and sleep and comforting touch, she was less tuned in to Millie's emotional states. Millie herself was a pale, thin, and under-powered baby: she conveyed little confidence that she could attract and hold her mother's attention. Instead, Kirstie seemed to dominate their encounters with her own need for recognition. She pinched Millie on the cheek and when Millie looked away from her, she loudly and persistently demanded that Millie should "look at Mummy".

At three months, there were already questions about the way the relationship might develop. Kirstie's obvious affection for Millie was no guarantee that she would be able to empathise with Millie's emotional experience. As our work continued, it soon became much clearer that Kirstie had little sense of Millie as a separate person with feelings of her own. She rarely played with Millie at home, or engaged with her face to face. More often, she left her lying in the corridor while she did her chores, or had her on her lap when she watched her favourite TV programmes late into the night. Although she did respond to Millie if she was really distressed, she seemed to resent Millie's demands for ordinary attention or play, and at these moments would complain in a jokey way that Millie was a "bully and a terrorist".

To encourage Kirstie to become more aware of Millie's feelings, I asked her to practice the technique known as "watch, wait, and wonder" (Cohen et al., 1999) as Millie became more mobile and active. This involves watching the baby play, without adult participation—unless the child takes the initiative and invites a response from the parent. The aim is to observe patiently, and to reflect on the meaning of the child's own play.

Kirstie didn't manage this well. For her, it was torture simply to observe Millie. She had "itchy" fingers which longed to touch Millie. She desperately needed the constant physical contact with Millie to regulate and soothe *herself*, (not Millie). In effect, she was treating Millie as an extension of herself, using her projectively to meet her own unmet needs for regulation.

Kirstie couldn't bear Millie learning from her own mistakes and couldn't restrain her urge to take over the play and do it *for* Millie—the kind of intrusiveness characteristic of disorganised attachment—again, a failure to see the child as a separate person with her own wishes and emotions.

In fact, Kirstie found it quite baffling to be asked to "wonder" or to find symbolic or emotional meaning in Millie's play. When asked what she had noticed, she would describe Millie's physical actions in a rather literal and concrete way such as "then she picked up the rattle and put it in her mouth". She didn't see behind Millie's behaviour to the emotional drivers of that behaviour.

I began to understand why previous professionals had been so frustrated with her parenting, to the point where one treatment centre had declared her "untreatable" and incapable of mentalizing.

It was tempting to challenge Kirstie about her lack of interest in Millie. But how could Kirstie get inside Millie's mind when no-one had ever got inside hers?

Kirstie's sense of self was rather blank. Like so many people who have not had their emotions recognised and co-regulated in early life, she tried not to feel. There are many ways of defending against feeling such as splitting, projection, passive aggression, and compliance. Certainly at times, Kirstie seemed dissociated from her feelings and always had huge difficulty in putting them into words.

At the start of our work, Kirstie was not aware of the connections between her early life and her current difficulties in relating to others (she was extremely isolated and had an unsatisfactory marriage to an older man who came and went as he pleased). She had few memories of childhood and little awareness of the way her life had evolved. Most of the relational experiences she did remember were about physical contact, such as sharing a bed with her mother, and food—the things that she now provided for Millie. She assumed it was normal for children to be left on their own for most of the day, without playmates, as she had been. Her mother had worked long hours and came back late in the evening, when she disappeared into the kitchen to cook for herself. She idealised her parents, but was afraid of both of them, since they punished her with both verbal and physical abuse when she made any demands of her own, or displeased them in any way, convincing her that she must be basically bad. These neglectful, unempathic, and rejecting early experiences made it hard for Kirstie to develop an accurate self narrative—presumably why the coherent narrative is such a marker of attachment security.

Parent state of mind shapes baby's state of mind

As Kirstie and I established a regulatory therapeutic attachment and started to build a more empathic self narrative that made sense of her unconscious emotional patterns, the work quite rapidly started to bear fruit. As her self-awareness grew, she became less socially phobic and fearful of other people and started to engage with other parents in a local playgroup. She also became more aware of Millie's states of mind, and Millie started to become more lively and able to explore. But people are part of wider relational systems, too. As Kirstie got more confident, her husband felt threatened. He was unfaithful and they separated.

At this crisis point, her mother—now retired—decided to come to live with her and help her with the children. Despite her growing self-awareness, Kirstie's sense of self was not yet strong enough to challenge the relationship patterns she had grown up with, of being ignored and undervalued. Her mother took over the tasks Kirstie most enjoyed—the cooking, and even most of the mothering of Millie too. Her occasional violent outbursts made Kirstie fearful and passive, and unable to think—the learned helplessness of the traumatised (to which Dr Sandra Bloom refers in her chapter in this volume (Bloom, 2013).

Our work in the therapy stalled. Kirstie became depressed, switched off from her feelings and fell back into an old compliant narrative from her childhood of "I owe everything to my mother and as a good Christian I must obey her". It felt like all the work we had done to understand her life was being unravelled. Kirstie's impotence became mine.

And it became Millie's too. At ten months old, she seemed to be under stress. She was increasingly fretful, seemed uncomfortable in her skin, and sometimes slept in sessions, which she had rarely done before. During this period, Millie's play became strikingly passive. She only explored the toys within easy reach, and rarely made any demands for interaction. She seemed to have gone into suspended animation. It seemed as if her developing self couldn't flourish without her mother's emotional responsiveness and empathy.

There isn't an entirely happy ending to this story. For several months we hung in there, trying to process the distress, but we were really stuck. It was challenging for me to maintain empathy with Kirstie in her cut-off state, week after week. I found it increasingly hard to think and reflect, and my supervision group felt hopeless too. In the midst of all this I had to go away for three months on sabbatical, knowing when I returned we would soon be facing the end of our clinical time together as Millie approached her second birthday.

When I returned, I discovered Kirstie had found her own solution to the impasse. She had turned to a new man, Pete, someone who seemed much more able to sustain her emotionally than her previous husband. This triggered a huge fight with her mother, who tried to force her to give him up. But the power of the new sexual relationship gave Kirstie the courage to ask her mother to move out, the most active display of agency I had ever seen from her.

Millie, too, had seized the opportunity to relate to this warm, child-friendly man who gave her lots of attention. She had become rapidly attached to Pete and often protested to see Pete go when he dropped them off at the session. By the time of our last few weeks in therapy together, Millie was playing more freely and expressing herself more forcefully. Her increased physical mobility helped her to do this with some gusto. Sometimes she threw toys around, and one time got angry in a session when she could not reach the tap on the basin that attracted her. Her development seemed to have resumed and she was becoming a more visible "self".

However, Millie's growing autonomy made Kirstie feel rejected. She still wanted continuous close physical contact with Millie to soothe and reassure herself. But it was a real step forward that Kirstie was now able to recognise that this was her need and not Millie's. She had also become much more able to identify her complicated feelings about both her mother and Pete, as well as to experience, with me, a real sadness at the loss of our relationship. Kirstie's own emotional development and greater capacity to empathise with Millie could now pave the way for her baby's emotional development.

Overcoming resistance to empathy

Although I have chosen to describe a mother and baby dyad, I believe the same issues are at the heart of individual work in psychotherapy.

To illustrate this briefly, I will describe a fragment of Malcolm's psychotherapy, taken from the beginning of a long and eventually fruitful therapeutic relationship. Malcolm was a middle-aged man who had a similar story to Kirstie, in the sense that he had grown up with a punitive, emotionally unresponsive parent. His fears of being hurt by other people made him even more resistant to the therapeutic process than Kirstie, who was at least motivated to do the best for her baby. Sometimes he would complain bitterly that therapy was all a waste of time, other times he was silent for long periods. Like so many clients who have had previous relationships which were painful, traumatic and distressing, Malcolm had a variety of defences—ranging from emotional avoidance and withdrawal to hyper-sensitivity, blaming and rejecting—which not only didn't *invite* attunement or empathy, but often seemed designed to repel it.

I understood my early work with Malcolm in the light of the same three key developmental processes that had directed my work with Kirstie and Millie: first, to build a therapeutic alliance, second to identify his current emotions and to regard them in a kindly and accepting light so they could be regulated, and third, to construct a self narrative that made sense of his emotional experiences over time. All three, in my view, require empathy to be effective.

Like a mother with a new baby, I wanted Malcolm to know that I was trying to read his emotional states moment by moment, and wanting to engage with him in a turn-taking dialogue so that we could start to understand each other. Using an approach not unlike "watch, wait, and wonder", I would tune in as acutely as I could, and give him feedback on the smallest movements of emotion that I observed. I would say things like: "You looked as if you had something you wanted to express just then, but you gave up on expressing it", or: "You give me the sense that that thought upset you?", or: "You conveyed a real excitement then when you were talking about your piano playing".

Malcolm sometimes conveyed a profound and icy indifference or hostility towards me. This behaviour had an impact on me. I felt unsure what he needed, and like the first mother I described, I sometimes found myself getting tense and anxious. In other words, my own emotional regulation would wobble.

Research has established that one of the main obstacles to empathy is the caregiver's own difficulty in regulating herself, as we saw with Kirstie, who used physical contact with Millie as a way of holding herself together but could not put herself in Millie's shoes because of her lack of self-awareness. In order to regulate *myself*, I needed to maintain my self-awareness and to gather up my own inner resources, so that I could make the *effort* to empathise with Malcolm and to mentalize about what was going on for him.

But this wasn't an easy option. It involved a real investment of energy and imagination, to give priority to feeling with him as best as I could. It didn't mean thinking loving thoughts or trying to be nice. So often the emotions with which clients most need help are those which are the hardest to enter into and process—a baby's distress, a child's bullying behaviour, a client's envy, hatred, guilt, and fear. Some therapists may try to regulate their own negative responses by creating a critical distance from the client. I felt it was more challenging to attempt to imagine myself into Malcolm's feelings of hostility towards myself.

The more I immersed myself in Malcolm's state of mind, the more my thoughts would also turn to wondering and reflecting what was motivating Malcolm's hostility—perhaps his implicit assumptions formed in infancy that others would be as hostile and indifferent to his dependency needs as his mother had been? Or perhaps some current interactions—either with myself or others—which had triggered his feeling of anger and disappointment?

Sometimes it seemed as if my wordless internal activity alone was enough—and the emotional atmosphere would become more benign without anything being said. Certainly I felt that, although there were many currents of transference and countertransference in play between us, interpreting them mattered less than Malcolm experiencing a relationship which was not dominated by the caregiver's needs. By remaining emotionally available, empathic, and non-judgemental even whilst he was rejecting me, Malcolm was getting a powerful implicit message that the relationship would not collapse under his negative feelings—actually, all feelings were safe to feel.

The empathic narrative

Of course there were many occasions when our relationship needed more overt verbal repair, and certainly words also play an essential role in communicating understanding. In the early days of a baby's life, this communication is a basic process of identifying and naming feelings. But as the child's sense of self becomes more complex, the caregiver's words and feedback of his perceptions of the child's behavioural patterns play a crucial role in helping the child to construct a narrative of self, an enduring sense of self over time. But this, too, can be done empathically or unempathically, and the same is true of psychotherapy.

There is a danger of framing the client's unconscious patterns in an unempathic way. For example, a therapist may describe a problem in a judgemental way, telling the client: "You avoid sexual feelings"—a statement which is likely to reinforce the client's conviction that he is inadequate or unworthy whilst the therapist herself is superior. Alternatively, a more empathic therapist might say: "You seem rather harsh with yourself when you sense any hint of sexual feeling" (Bohart, 1997)—a statement which keeps the client within the safety of an empathic "we" relationship, inviting the client to process difficult feelings together *with* the therapist.

People who have not experienced a secure base with their early attachment figure may have never experienced this feeling of being part of a regulatory "we". But without it, how can anyone develop a secure base inside the self? Clients who start from a lifetime of insecure attachment experiences "earn" attachment security primarily from learning to trust in another person's empathic responsiveness. Slowly, this changes the internal landscape. It builds up new neural structures and enables more effective ways of self-regulating.

Equally important, empathic re-framing of the individual's implicit patterns of relating can undo some of the trauma of past mistreatment and create a more positive self narrative.

Reinforcing the positive

New ways of working with parents and babies have begun to highlight the importance of building such positive experiences as well as processing past traumas. Parent infant psychotherapy is eclectic and in many ways at the cutting edge of psychotherapy. It is constantly adapting to new information from developmental psychology and neurobiology. Less weighed down by past theory and tradition, it is open to new techniques, and there is a refreshing focus on "what works?"

In a new technique called video interaction guidance (VIG), parents are supported and encouraged to build a positive alliance with the therapist. Once this is established, interactions with their child are videoed so that they can be reflected on with the therapist. But instead of focusing on the negative parenting behaviours on display, the technique is about deliberately helping parents to recognise instances of good relating, to enable them to notice what *positive* relationships look like. The technique implicitly acknowledges that many parents have missed out on sensitive, responsive, empathic parenting in their own early lives, and will need help to develop their relational capacities and responsiveness to others.

Looking at the video material together, the therapist highlights every example where the parent has demonstrated the relational skills of turn-taking, of eye contact, of tuning in to the nuances of their child's feelings, as well as of staying in touch with their own (different) feelings. The goal is to open the door to try out new, more successful, ways of relating to others and to reinforce positive skills as they emerge. This experience, with its visual "proof" of skilful relating, is proving enormously successful in helping to build a parent's self-esteem and confidence in their relational abilities.

Equally, I have come to think that it is vital in adult psychotherapy to build up the client's sense of lovability and to make them more aware of their strengths. People like Kirstie and Malcolm not only need acceptance and reflective understanding of their current emotions such as shame or rage, but also to feel they have a place "in the heart of the other", as Diana Fosha, (2000, pp. 58–89), puts it, in her magnificent book on the transforming power of affect, a book which has profoundly influenced my clinical work. Clients need their therapist to recognise the *value* of their unique qualities and personal history, so that they can develop their missing positive sense of self.

This can be just as much of a challenge to the client as processing trauma. However negative their implicit relational patterns of infancy have been, at least they have been *reliably* negative. As Fosha says, clients may fear that recognising their own competence can mean letting go of the hope of ever receiving the emotional care that has been missing in life. Even being appreciated for one's qualities can feel dangerous; what if the appreciation is withdrawn? When I had an opportunity to notice and point out an improvement in Malcolm's relationship with his partner, or with one of his colleagues, or to draw attention to his sense of humour or a particular talent he had just revealed, I did so. Yet Malcolm seemed both to love this feedback and to hate it. It helped build a narrative of a positive self that had been missing, but at the same time, it could be painful—as Fosha says: "having is a reminder of not-having." (2000, p. 177).

Building the positives doesn't imply a Pollyanna-ish denial of the negative. Conflicts and misunderstandings arise in any and every close relationship, and anyone can become defensive when their equilibrium is threatened.

But it is so important that the client isn't re-traumatised by being judged in a negative light or held at arm's length as with the mother and baby I started with in this paper. Empathy is so important because it gets alongside negative feelings, to really understand the client's experiences from the inside. It goes further than attunement, which is more about the immediate present—drawing on sensitivity and responsiveness to regulate current emotion. Empathy is a response to the whole individual. It is about grasping the uniqueness of the individual and being aware of his or her personal history through time.

In particular, an empathic narrative recognises that it is not the client who is negative, but the *relationships* that the client has experienced in the past, and the relational patterns that he or she has internalised. Therapy based on modern developmental understanding recognises that our selves are really the emergent properties of actual relationships. Self doesn't exist outside of relationships. As Sandra Bloom puts it in her chapter in this volume, "without attachment there is no human being." (Bloom, 2013). Each individual self is forged in early one-to one-exchanges, and is elaborated over time, nested in wider circles of social relationships rippling out to society as a whole.

This more relational perspective makes it clear that the twentieth century style of psychotherapy, as a power relationship where the superior therapist tries to force the patient to grow up, is as outdated and unhelpful as parenting which insists on deference to authority and overly strict disciplinary practices. In the twenty-first century, many societies are becoming more democratic. The world is more interconnected. Increasingly people's working lives are about communication, not about clocking on and off in a factory. We need to relate better to each other. All this has influenced what we might call "the relational turn" in psychotherapy and the need to understand each other in more depth—which makes empathy more important than ever.

That doesn't mean empathy is easy. Although it is one of our most distinctive human abilities—being able to understand what other people are feeling, and being willing to enter into other people's pain and difficulty as well as their joys—its presence in human culture can't be taken for granted. It is something we can only pass on to others when we have experienced it ourselves. Many people have not experienced empathic relationships. They don't know how to give or receive empathy. This can make them difficult to empathise with. It is certainly not a soft option. But just as the *individual*'s quality of life, and ability to achieve earned security, depends on it—so too does our *collective* quality of life depend on the giving and receiving of empathy.

References

Bloom, S. (2013). Creating, destroying and restoring Sanctuary within caregiving organisations. In: *From Broken Attachments to Earned Security: The Role of Empathy in Therapeutic Change*. London: Karnac.

Bohart, A. (1997). *Empathy Reconsidered: New Directions in Psychotherapy*. A. C. Bohart, & L. S. Greenberg (Eds.). Washington, D.C.: APA.

Cohen, N. J., Muir, E., Lojkasek, M., Muir, R., Parker, J. P., Barwick, M., & Brown, M. (1999). Watch, wait, and wonder: Testing the effectiveness of a new approach to mother–infant psychotherapy. *Infant Mental Health Journal, 20(4)*: 429–451.

Decety, J. (2011). Dissecting the neural mechanisms mediating empathy. *Emotion Review, 3(1)*: 92–108.

Fosha, D. (2000). *The Transforming Power of Affect*. New York: Basic Books.

Freud, S. (1912e). Recommendations to physicians practising psycho–analysis, *S. E., 12*: 111–120. London: Hogarth.

Gerhardt, S. (2010). *The Selfish Society*. London: Simon & Schuster.

Klein, J. (1995). *Doubts and Certainties in the Practice of Psychotherapy*. London: Karnac.

Knox, J. (2011). *Self Agency in Psychotherapy*. London: Norton and Co.

Samuels, A. (1996). From sexual misconduct to social justice. In: *Psychoanalytic Dialogues, 6*: 295–321.

Schore, A., & Schore, J. (2008). Modern attachment theory: The central role of affect regulation in development and treatment. In: *Clinical Social Work Journal, 36*: 9–20.

Stern, D. (1985). *The Interpersonal World of the Infant*. London: Karnac.

CHAPTER THREE

Love bombing: a simple self-help intervention for parents to reset their child's emotional thermostat

Oliver James

Introduction

The "love bombing" method is a simple way to help parents to reduce a wide variety of problem behaviours in their offspring aged from three to early puberty. It does so by giving the child a condensed, intense experience of feeling that their attachment needs are being met, sometimes through encouraging the child to regress to a toddler. Whilst the method has never been subjected to a controlled study, thousands of parents have now carried it out. Of these, I have personally had feedback about the results from approximately two hundred parents, nearly all of them positive.

In this paper, I will explain the theoretical background of the method before providing a brief account of it, as I explain it to parents.

In summary, I believe that the method rebalances cortisol levels in the child and enables them to move from an anxious to a secure pattern of attachment.

The background

The main theoretical basis for love bombing is, on the one hand, the proposition that genes appear to play little role—remarkably little—in explaining why one sibling is different to another. On the other hand, there is a substantial body of evidence that early nurture plays a critical role in setting what I term a "child's emotional thermostat": its consistent patterns of levels of key chemicals, like neurotransmitters, and its brain waves.

If it is true that childhood electro-chemistry is largely set by nurture, it might be possible to alter that "thermostatic" setting by changing the pattern of nurture. Love bombing suggests that remarkably little time spent engaging in a different, more benign way of relating to the child is required.

It is far beyond the scope of this paper to supply much detail for any of the contentions herein, but in what follows, I shall briefly set out the key arguments and refer to a few key scientific sources. In discussing the role of nurture in affecting a child's electro-chemistry, I shall use the example of the hormone, cortisol.

The role of genes

For decades it has been confidently asserted by mainstream psychiatrists and psychologists that genes are a major determinant of personality traits, mental ability and psychopathology. The assertions were supported by studies of identical twins.

Following the completion of the mapping of the human genome at the turn of the century, it was forcefully predicted that the specific genes for specific traits would be identified. However, the molecular geneticists who have carried out the human genome project now admit that they have been unable to explain almost any of the variance in traits through either individual genes or groups thereof. This lack of findings is characterised by them as "missing heritability" or "the DNA deficit". Whilst the search for the errant genes continues, there are strong grounds for doubting that it will succeed.

For many years the validity of twin studies has been questioned (James, 2002; Joseph, 2003). Whilst there is great reluctance to consider the possibility, it seems very possible that the true interpretation of greater similarity between identical rather than non-identical twins is actually an effect of the identical twins receiving more similar nurture. This is largely uncontested by geneticists but they maintain that the reason identical twins are more similarly nurtured is because they elicit more similar care by their inborn traits. This interpretation is becoming less and less tenable in the light of the findings of the Human Genome Project: at least seven hundred studies have been conducted of over sixty illnesses of all kinds, yet only a tiny number of physical ones, like certain breast cancers, have been demonstrated to be substantially explicable by genes. In nearly all studies of DNA individual genes or groups thereof can explain less than five per cent of the variance in the trait under scrutiny. As Joseph has argued persuasively (2013), it is increasingly looking as if the null hypothesis of the Human Genome Project will have to be accepted: genes play very little role in explaining individual difference.

An interesting implication of that finding would be that it is not any inborn psychological traits of identical twins which elicit more similar nurture, but simply their similarities in appearance. Even more significant, if genes do not fix our psychopathologies, then the potential for much greater plasticity and for therapeutic interventions which nurture this, could be far greater than previously supposed.

The role of nurture in causing electro-chemical patterns in children: the example of cortisol

Cortisol is the hormone secreted when a person is experiencing threat. It causes the "fight or flight" response. Although the theory has not been tested, my hypothesis is that love bombing rebalances a child's cortisol levels, along with other hormones and neurotransmitters.

There is abundant evidence that abnormal cortisol levels are found in maltreated children with a wide variety of mental illnesses (Tarullo & Gunnar, 2006). Abnormal cortisol is common in children (Denson, Spanovic & Miller, 2009) and adults with anxious patterns of attachment (Shaver, 2007). There is also persuasive evidence that childhood maltreatment causes cortisol abnormalities which result in neurological deficits in adults, expressed as mental illnesses, particularly the symptoms associated with post traumatic stress disorder (PTSD) (Teicher, Andersen, Polcari, Anderson, Navalta & Kim, 2003).

There is now a large body of evidence that early nurture profoundly affects cortisol levels in children (Hunter et al., 2011). This starts before birth. Several studies have demonstrated that maternal stress in the last trimester of pregnancy is associated with postnatal cortisol dysregulation (Sarkar, Bergman, O'Connor & Glover, 2008), continuing to exert an independent effect into childhood, including raised risk of attention deficit hyperactivity disorder (ADHD) (O'Connor, Heron, Golding, Beveridge & Glover, 2002); (O'Connor, Ben-Shlomo, Heron, Golding, Adams & Glover, 2005).

Once born, the responsiveness of the main carer to the infant has a strong effect on cortisol secretion. One study repays close inspection (Hibel, Granger, Blair & Cox, 2011). It had a sample of 1,100 mothers and babies who were measured for maternal sensitivity to the infant at seven, fifteen, and twenty four months of age. At each of those ages the babies were exposed to briefly stressful challenges. For example, at seven months, the infants were given an attractive toy to play with for thirty seconds. The experimenter then placed the toy just beyond the infant's reach behind a clear plastic container. This was repeated twice more. Similar challenges were carried out at fifteen and twenty four months.

Swabs of saliva were taken from the child before and after the challenges on each occasion to measure cortisol. This identified how stressed the child was at the outset and how quickly it recovered from being challenged, its reactivity.

In addition, the amount of physical violence by either parent towards the other was measured for the previous twelve months at each assessment. Other factors which might affect the child, like maternal depression, were also assessed.

The results showed that exposure to parental violence did not affect how reactive the child was to the challenges at either seven or fifteen months, but it did at age two. The accumulation of exposure to violence primed the child to become reactive—the more they had been exposed at all three ages, the more their cortisol levels jumped when challenged at twenty four months, and the longer it took for them to settle down afterwards.

But the most interesting finding was that maternal sensitivity at seven months was a crucial factor in the reaction at age two. Children whose mothers were very sensitive in the first year but who had also witnessed high levels of violence were still calm when challenged at age two. The good early care meant their cortisol levels were indistinguishable from babies who had had no exposure to parental violence.

Furthermore, high maternal responsiveness at fifteen months and age two did not have the same protective effect. If the seven month care had not been responsive, then even if subsequent care was provided, the toddler was highly reactive if there had been parental violence. Early responsiveness had a powerful protective effect.

Another telling study explored the mechanisms explaining why children have differential cortisol reactions to parental disharmony (El-Sheikh, Kouros, Erath, Cummings, Keller & Staton, 2009). Children exposed to repeated parental conflict have been shown to react physically. Their heart rates, the sweatiness of their hands, their sleep patterns, and their cortisol levels are all affected. However, the new study examined more sophisticated bodily reactions.

Our physical responses to the environment are primarily expressed through the sympathetic and parasympathetic nervous systems. Put crudely, the sympathetic nervous system (SNS) stimulates "fight or flight" when faced with perceived threats, preparing us for action—reactions like diverting blood from the gut to the muscles, faster breathing, and raised heart beat. Conversely, the parasympathetic nervous system (PNS) prepares the body to "rest and digest", to "chill out"—more blood for the guts, slower breathing.

Past studies examined the relationship between various stressors, including parental conflict, and either the SNS or the PNS separately. The new study looked at the joint effect on both systems at the same time.

It found that children developed externalising behaviour in response to parental conflict if both PNS and SNS were simultaneously switched on. If the "fight or flight" responses were going full blast with the "rest and digest" doing the same, the child was liable to be reported by parents and teachers as prone to externalising.

This was because the SNS system seems to override the PNS, the child becoming angry, even chaotically furious, and getting involved in fights with parents, who then start using extreme measures to control the child, up to and including hitting. The pattern now established, the child takes it to school, with teachers reporting them to be more liable to fight, disrupt classes and be prone to inattention.

Equally, if the child's response to parental conflict was for both systems to shut down, it was unable to produce adequate emotional responses, neither reacting actively nor chilled. Instead it goes into a state of passive vigilance, leaving it wide open to the nasty scenes and unable to express its distress or anger. Such children were more prone to delinquency and inattention at home and school.

By contrast, when the children reacted by either one or other system going into action, they were much less likely to externalise. They seemed to be protected by active coping responses, like becoming healthily distressed or keeping a safe distance but trying to calm everyone down.

Given the huge body of evidence showing that these electro-chemical systems are heavily influenced by nurture, from before birth onwards, when taken with the study reported above by Hibel, Granger, Blair, and Cox, it is highly probable that prior experiences (and not genes) establish the basic pattern with which they respond to later exposure to parental conflict.

As well as maternal responsiveness, the consistency and type of early care affects cortisol levels (James, 2010). For example seventy fifteen-month-old toddlers were observed on three occasions: at home before starting group daycare, during the time the mother left the daycare facility, and after the mother had gone (Ahnert, Gunnar, Lamb & Barthel, 2004). During the first hour after the mother had departed, cortisol levels almost doubled compared with the level when the toddler was measured at home before ever having experienced daycare. This increase after the first hour was also found on the fifth and ninth days of going to daycare. It is compelling evidence that in the short term, leaving a toddler in daycare dramatically increases their cortisol levels in the hour after the mother departs.

However, being left in a new situation and the disappearance of the mother might naturally make the toddler initially anxious. Perhaps the cortisol levels settled down once the toddler got used to the new place? When they were measured again after having attended daycare for five months, although the amount of the increase in cortisol compared with the original level at home had decreased, it was still significantly higher. This is but one of many studies suggesting that daycare has lasting effects on cortisol levels (James, 2010).

This brief account of some of the research regarding the impact of nurture on cortisol levels is highly pertinent to the possible mechanisms by which love bombing may have its effect. My hypothesis is that a great many of the troubled children who have been love bombed would have had elevated or blunted cortisol prior to the intervention and that measured afterwards, the experience would have "reset" them to more benign ones.

Love bombing

My full account of the method is provided in my book *Love Bombing—Reset your Child's Emotional Thermostat* (James, 2012a). It uses case histories to enable parents to identify the right way for them to apply it to their circumstances. Here, I shall restrict myself to reproducing a piece I wrote addressed to parents in the Guardian newspaper—I cannot better this, in aiming to give a condensed version:

In March 2010 I received an email from Miranda, a very worried mother. She wrote that her son Tim, then nine, "seems to not like himself and has no focus. He says he hates himself and that he's rubbish at everything". A bright boy, he refused to do his homework and was prone to temper tantrums.

The solution that I proposed is called love bombing, a method I developed to reset the emotional thermostats of children aged from three to puberty. It entails a period of time alone with your child, offering him or her unlimited love and control. It works for a wide variety of common problems, severe or mild, from defiant, even violent aggression, to shyness, trouble sleeping or underperformance at school.

This is not the same as "quality time", just hanging out with your child. When you love bomb, you create a special emotional zone wholly different from your normal life, with new rules. Over 100 families have now tried it, nearly all with positive results. It has spread virally on the internet (not to be confused with the love bombing done by cults). Google: "oliver james love bombing" and you will find thousands of pages.

So, how exactly does it work? First, you explain to your child that sometime soon, the two of you are going to spend time together and are going to have a lot of fun. Your child is going to decide what they want and when they want it, within reason. You give the message that this is going to be a big event: it's coming soon—how exciting! Your child then draws up a list. It doesn't matter if that includes lots of watching *Sponge Bob Squarepants*: the key is that it is your child who has chosen it.

Throughout the experience, you are trying, as much as possible, to give them the feeling of "Whatever I want, I get"—a very unusual one of being in control and of being gratified, as well as bombed with love.

You may be thinking, "Are you mad? My child is already a tyrant—rewarding him like that is just going to make it even worse!" This is quite understandable. Love bombing seems to fly in the face of conventional wisdom, which often recommends more control, not less, when a child is not complying, and stricter, firmer reactions to undesirable behaviour.

But the point is that the love bomb zone is separate from ordinary life. Out of that zone, you continue trying to set boundaries, consistently and firmly. In fact, the love bombing experience will feed back in a very benign way, greatly reducing the amount of time you spend imposing limits, nagging, and nattering—the "Don't do that", "I've told you before, put that down", "Leave your sister alone" into which all parents get sucked sometimes. And it's worth doing with almost any child, even happy ones will benefit.

A key practical decision you need to make at the outset is the length of time you will spend in the zone and the frequency. At one extreme, you can take your child away from the family home for a couple of nights at a hotel or bed and breakfast (or rent a cheap gypsy caravan, as one mother did).

Alternatively, as many parents have done, the rest of your family can spend the weekend with relatives or friends, leaving you at home with your child. There is absolutely no necessity to spend any money to do love bombing. Many parents have done a day away from home, or just bursts of a few hours.

In the case of Miranda and her depressed son Tim, as a dual-income family, they could afford two nights away at a cheap hotel. They settled in there on the Friday night and set off into town on the Saturday. Much of the time was spent just wandering around, a certain amount of shopping and a visit to an aquarium.

Miranda recalled that just this day "… made Tim feel very special, it definitely worked. I realise not everyone can afford a hotel and shopping. And anyway, when it came to spending money, Tim was reasonable about absolutely everything, much to my surprise." Children who feel loved are less consumption-obsessed.

After a peaceful Saturday night back in the hotel with Kentucky fried chicken and *The X Factor*, on Sunday they pottered around again, did some more shopping and visited a zoo on the way home.

As well as Tim feeling in control during this time, there was much affection expressed. Miranda recalls that "Tim spent a great deal of time cuddling up to me and telling me how much he loved me (always reciprocated). It was interesting for me not to be in charge. I do tend to lead. Here, it really was mostly Tim's decision what we did next, what we ate and what we watched on television."

In the guidelines I offer for love bombing, I suggest getting the child to give the experience a name before doing it, like "special time" or "mummy time". Often it helps for them to have received a material object to remind them of the experience, like a stone from a beach or a teddy. Using this and the name to help as prompts, when on returning, parents are asked to try and carve out half an hour an evening when they can briefly re-enter the love bomb zone together, even if it's only to watch some television.

Miranda has two other children and for various reasons that proved difficult. Instead, she says: "I give Tim random bits of time and have recently taken to holding and cuddling him like a baby and even saying to him 'You're my baby boy and I love you.'" You have to customise the method to suit your circumstances and the problems you and your child are experiencing.

The impact of the love bombing weekend was immediate and dramatic. Five weeks afterwards, Miranda wrote to me that "Overall he is happier. He still has tantrums, but since the weekend away I haven't heard him say that he hates himself at all—not once, come to think of it." Eighteen months later, she reported that "It is getting better largely due to the love bombing and subsequent changes in our relationship."

I have had very similar reports of sustained success—followed up one to two years after the love bombing—from parents helping children with violent aggression, myriad anxiety problems, attention deficit hyperactivity disorder (ADHD), sleeplessness, perfectionism and even autism.

In many cases, I suspect that the experience stabilises levels of the fight–flight hormone cortisol. If too high, the child can be manic or aggressive or anxious, if too low,—blunted—the child may be listless or surly.

Even a brief experience of love and control seems to correct that. Recent evidence suggests that children are far more plastic than was once thought and that the way they are is not fixed in our genes for the vast majority of problems.

The love bombing zone need not be a whole weekend. For instance, in the case of three-year-old Sam, he seemed a lot more sensitive than his younger brother, easily overwhelmed by simple situations. Sometimes he would melt down in toddler-like rages. He got very jumpy when separated from his mother, Emma. She said that: "In the house, he wants to know where I am all the time". If she was upstairs and he was downstairs he would scream asking her whereabouts.

For practical reasons, she planned two consecutive love bombing Saturdays away from home with him, rather than a night. The first was named "pirate day" by him because they went to a funfair. He adored feeling in control and the expressions of love.

As recommended by my protocol of what to do, she told him that she loved him repeatedly. Initially, she made a point of looking at her watch every fifteen minutes or so and then telling him. Once into the habit, she just continued.

Since that day they find it easier to frequently express love. She believes they now have "Much, much better communication." She also says "It was good fun, a great day that reminded us of the good times that we can have together, setting us back on that track. It was a truly lovely day." Often it is not just the child's thermostat that is corrected, it is also the parent's thermostat in relation to the child. After love bombing many parents report feeling it has been the first time for months or years when they remembered how much they love them.

The second day was based at home and included a complete meltdown by him. It is extremely common during love bombing for the child to test out if the parent is for real—really loves them or will still love them if they are horrible. Emma rode it out and they emerged much closer.

Afterwards, she reported that "He has not had any unreachable tantrums since that one on the last love bombing day, four weeks ago." What is more, his fear of not knowing where she is in the house has disappeared.

Whatever the child's actual age, it can help to think of them as an eighteen-month-old when in the love bombing zone. Parents have reported that their child has brief periods during the love bombing when they actually revert to being like a toddler, cuddling and even using baby talk. This is exactly what you are aiming for. You are trying to give them the chance to go back to earlier periods, but this time it is really, really good; they feel totally safe, loved and in control.

Many parents have shown great ingenuity in adapting the method to their circumstances or problems. For example, four-year-old Jeff was having terrible temper tantrums, sometimes directed against his two-year-old sister. His mother Carole introduced twice or thrice weekly "time in charge sessions", as Jeff named them. These entailed Carole being led in play by Jeff.

A basic game was running races which mummy had to join in with, holding the baby, charging round the room. However, by far the majority of the time was taken up with fantasy play.

Some were open-ended scenarios, in which imaginary babies would transform into fishes and back again. More commonly, there would be specific narratives that progressed according to his script, sometimes dream-like. He particularly enjoyed disasters, like sinking ships, with his mother and daughter employed in a variety of supporting roles.

The impact of this version of love bombing was dramatic. Carole reported that: "Immediately after we started the play sessions the temper tantrums stopped. There were just no incidents any more of a significant nature. That has been true for three months now."

However you do love bombing, there is nothing to lose. What's not to like about spending some time having fun with your child? If it transforms them and your relationship, so much the better, but the worst that can happen is you return from the zone having had a good time. (James, 2012b)

Since the publication of the above article, and of the book, I have received about one hundred emails from parents informing me of the benign consequences of using the method with a wide variety of problems. As well as reporting that the child's problems decreased, nearly all state that they attribute this to a lasting alteration in their pattern of relating.

Conclusion

There is a growing consensus that the medical model of mental illness is not supported by scientific evidence. A recent statement by the British Psychological Society's division of clinical psychology asserted that the genetic and neuroscientific evidence for psychiatric diagnoses is insufficient to merit their continued use (*The Observer* (Guardian Media Group), 2013). Instead of labelling children or adults with mental illnesses, they propose that we concentrate on the psychosocial causes of distress.

For decades, attachment researchers and practitioners have been arguing that early care is a vital factor in understanding and treating emotional distress. The scientific evidence now strongly supports this view. The news that genes play little part in causing it and that nurture in the early years plays a critical role is leading to a radical rethink of how we respond to troubled children and adults. In this chapter I have offered an account of a simple self-help method for rebalancing cortisol levels and fostering a secure attachment. There are numerous other interventions which show similar promise.

It is to be hoped that the next decade will see a rapid shift away from the widespread use of drugs to treat emotional distress in children. It is to be hoped that attachment-based interventions will play a big part in replacing them.

References

Ahnert, L., Gunnar, M. R., Lamb, M. E., & Barthel, M. (2004). Transition to child care: Associations with infant–mother attachment, infant negative emotion, and cortisol elevations. *Child Development, 75*: 639–650.

Denson, T. F., Spanovic, M., & Miller, N. (2009). Cognitive appraisals and emotions predict cortisol and immune responses: A meta-analysis of acute laboratory social stressors and emotion inductions. *Psychological Bulletin, 135*: 823–853.

El-Sheikh, M., Kouros, C. D., Erath, S., Cummings, E. M., Keller, P., & Staton, L. (2009). Marital conflict and children's externalizing behavior: Interactions between parasympathetic and sympathetic nervous system activity. *Monographs of the Society for Research in Child Development, 74(1)*: 1–79.

Hibel, L. C., Granger, D. A., Blair, C., Cox, M. J., & The Key Family Life Project Investigators. (2011). Maternal sensitivity buffers the adrenocortical implications of intimate partner violence exposure during early childhood. *Development and Psychopathology, 23*: 689–701.

Hunter, A. L., Minnis, H., & Wilson, P. (2011). Altered stress responses in children exposed to early adversity: A systematic review of salivary cortisol studies. *Stress, 14*: 614–626.

James, O. W. (2002). *They F*** You Up*. London: Bloomsbury.

James, O. W. (2010). *How Not To F*** Them Up*. London: Vermilion.

James, O. W. (2012a). *Love Bombing—Reset Your Child's Emotional Thermostat*. London: Karnac.

James, O. W. (2012b). All you need is love bombing. London: Guardian Newspaper, 22 September. Available at: www.theguardian.com/lifeandstyle/2012/sep/22/oliver-james-love-bombing-children.

Joseph, J. (2003). *The Gene Illusion*. London: PCCS Books.

Joseph, J. (2013). The missing heritability of psychiatric disorders: Elusive genes or non-existent genes? *Applied Developmental Science, 16*: 65–83.

O'Connor, T. G., Heron, J., Golding, J., Beveridge, M., & Glover, V. (2002). Maternal ante-natal anxiety and children's behavioural/emotional problems at 4 years. Report from the Avon Longitudinal Study of Parents and Children. *British Journal of Psychiatry, 180*: 502–508.

O'Connor, T. G., Ben-Shlomo, Y., Heron, J., Golding, J., Adams, D., & Glover, V. (2005). Prenatal anxiety predicts individual differences in cortisol in pre-adolescent children. *Biological Psychiatry, 58*: 211–217.

Sarkar, P., Bergman, K., O'Connor, T. G., & Glover, V. (2008). Maternal antenatal anxiety and amniotic fluid cortisol and testosterone: Possible implications for foetal programming. *Journal of Neuroendochrinology, 20*: 489–496.

Shaver, P. S. (2007). Adult attachment theory and the regulation of emotion. In: J. Gross, & R. A. Thompson (Eds.). *Handbook of Emotional Regulation* (pp. 446–465). New York: Guildford Press.

Tarullo, A. R., & Gunnar, M. R. (2006). Child maltreatment and the developing HPA axis. *Hormones and Behaviour, 50*: 632–639.

Teicher, M. H., Andersen, S. L., Polcari, A., Anderson, C. M., Navalta, C. P., & Kim, D. M. (2003). The neurobiological consequences of early stress and childhood maltreatment. *Neuroscience and Biobehavioral Reviews, 27*: 33–44.

The Observer (Guardian Media Group), (2013). Medicine's big new battleground: Does mental illness really exist?: 12th May 2013. Available at: www.guardian.co.uk/society/2013/may/12/medicine-dsm5-row-does-mental-illness-exist.

CHAPTER FOUR

To shed what still attempts to cling as if attached by thorns

Jane Haynes and Harry Whitehead

I chose this title because Rilke was a poet distinguished by his attraction to everything psychological and who lived in terror of being "unanswered": "Who, if I cried out among the angels' hierarchy would hear me?" (Rilke, 1981, p. 151).

Throughout his life Rilke raged against his mother's selfish vanities, which superseded any positive attachment to her infant son. Rilke went on sensationally to abandon his own wife and infant daughter in order to pursue artistic vision.

The patient I am writing about is called Harry, and he has written an accompanying version of moments in our long therapy, that is included below. He had a beautiful mother called Coral, who was an iconic figure in one of the first television soaps after the war: it is also important to add that she changed careers mid-pathway and opened an independent children's home. When Harry talked about her my involuntary thoughts conjured a siren on a protrusion of coral, holding not a comb but a mirror, smoothing auburn locks. Rilke's clinging thorns were imagistic of Harry's inappropriate attachment: by which I mean an ambivalent attachment that was—throughout the majority of our therapy—characterised by longing. His father had been one of the coolest and hippest members of the sixties underground and his work

41

is still celebrated by the National Film Theatre. He was also falconer to the Saudi Arabian royal family and his photographed image reveals him as gloriously handsome. His parents separated before Harry was born.

Harry was suffocating in an intellectual and emotional dependency on their equally famous and iconic lives, both of which were marked by a stunning and destructive narcissism, which left Harry living only in their shadows. Before long we agreed on one thing: Harry, whose psychic and physical body, his self, was a body in pain, needed a Parentectomy.

Before I continue the case history I want to make a deviation, which may also feel like a perversion in view of the conference title, and to confess how over worked, fatally under experienced, and over discussed I find that the concept of empathy has become among psychotherapists; although I have no intention of throwing out the baby with the bathwater.

Empathy, frequently conflated with sympathy or compassion, signifies a process of emotional and psychological projection. More specifically, outside of therapeutic jargon, it can refer to the concept of *Einfühlung*—literally, the activity of "feeling into"—that was developed in late-nineteenth-century Germany in the overlapping fields of philosophical aesthetics, perceptual psychology, and art and architectural history to describe an embodied response to an image, object, or spatial environment. Examples of projections into inanimate objects feel appropriate to me but when it comes to one person feeling, or worse, projecting their way into another psyche, I come unstuck. The best we can do is to educate and induce society towards an empathetic attitude, which I understand as caring about one's neighbour. I am comforted by Jung's position echoed by many of the greatest thinkers in various disciplines who are preoccupied by our solipsistic fate. "Philosophical criticism has helped me to see that every psychology—my own included—has the character of a subjective confession, even when I am dealing with empirical data, I am necessarily speaking about myself." (Nagy, 1991, p. 126). One of the most problematic aspects of any psychotherapy is the danger of therapists overestimating their powers of empathy when, in reality they are speaking at some unconscious or even conscious level, of themselves. Jung, on this occasion went on to say we can never know what the other is thinking and the best we can ever do is to respect their difference.

I can appreciate the therapeutic value of an empathetic attitude, so long as it does not indicate the ability to enter into another person's mind but only to imply a subjective estimation of another person's emotional inscape. Otherwise, I am content to work within the confines of a *sympathetic* attunement or engagement and I wonder why the idea of sympathy, despite its therapeutic origins and metaphors of wounds and healing, has become unfashionable. Engagement appeals to me with its symbolic commitment of therapist and patient collaborating to find and heal the source of dis-ease, a word whose meaning lies in its prefix "dis" to take away, ease or comfort.

The closest experience I have of clinical empathy is non-verbal and occurs in occasional golden moments between a patient arriving at the door and entering the room. In that split and language-less second, I may have divined or intuited more about how they are emotionally being/feeling in the world, which is not at all the same as accomplishing a shared understanding through fifty minutes of dialogue. If you were to ask me to put that cellular first impression into words it might, rather like the tissue of dreams, have disappeared before any cognition set in. Sometimes for the duration of a moment, I can see beyond the persona into an involuntary emotional "beingness" that I understand as the emotional inscape of the other. As soon as they take possession of the space, my consulting room, their animation, their resource to language, their persona becomes a defence against me reaching into their naked emotional and cellular vibrations of being.

If I concede to a therapeutic concept of an empathetic attitude in distinction to empathy, although I know that many people, both practitioners and patients long for it, I want to modify it by saying that it is precisely those patients who have suffered from failures of attachment and inconsistent caretaking in infancy who are most likely to be resistant to therapeutic attempts at an empathetic response, at least until the thorns of their narcissism shed. They may long to be emotionally understood, become angry when they inevitably feel they are not, but the idea of there being somebody to stand under them, *to understand*, can also feel like a heresy that may be perceived as an arrogant intrusion into self hood, which requires the slow growing roots of a collaborative and budding trust. These neglected children have often become attached to their own imagination and process of magical thinking. For those of us who have experienced traumatic attachment histories, the inevitability of thorny adhesions to our selfhood remain when childhood memories refuse to provide comfort to our adult selves or to reclaim the past with many pleasures. As an adult Rilke recalls night-time terrors of abandonment which you will soon hear echoed by Harry:

> But those fears that were my daily portion stirred a hundred other fears, and they arose in me and against me and banded together and I could not get beyond them. In striving to form them I became creative for them; instead of making them into things of my will I gave them a life of their own, and they turned that life against me and used it to pursue me far into the night. (Rilke, 2010)

The regressive nature of illness in particular can provoke more decaying thorns. Failures in infant attachment, with an accompanying likelihood of the individual's failure to develop efficient processes, or sometimes any process, of self soothing are often concealed behind states of hypochondriasis, for which I might suggest the challenging discipline of meditation running alongside of psychotherapy.

Harry, I discovered over several years, is among the most intellectually gifted people I have been privileged to know, but for years I was never sure if he was speaking truthfully. I found myself suspicious of his narrative, which is unusual, as I prefer to believe everything people share until it is proved otherwise. I suspected that he was exaggerating his cavalier academic successes, lying to himself and me. When he first arrived, and I still remember his punk hair and crumpled tee-shirt sporting some hip group, he was I think twenty-six going on fifteen. He told me that, after spending years in Thailand, he had returned to the United Kingdom (UK) where it seemed he dropped into Sussex University, and happened to pick up Japanese, "Well I knew Thai", and without doing much, except smoking weed, Harry went on, so he said, to pick up a first-class degree in Japanese and social anthropology. From the beginning of our therapy Harry had an obsession with the anthropologist Franz Boaz and the shaman Quesalid, who in another form was a Tlingit consultant to Boaz, called George Hunt. He would talk about these men and their shaman activities for session after session and such discussions left me feeling more confused, often useless, and wondering how to apply these shape movers to Harry's psychology. However, I could also see that he had found an erudite niche with which to impress, and that maybe one day this obsession might even form the basis of something greater than itself.

I pause to ask myself why I was suspicious of Harry's accounts of astonishing academic achievements, his pranks, fights, and conquests of Nepalese heights, Tibetan monasteries, and even his accounts of the radical back surgery and distressing medical incompetency he had submitted to before we met; but which over the years have all been shown to be true. I think it was because he seemed to shrink, in the extraordinary accounts of his parent's publicly archived lives; to lose oxygen, like in his asthma attacks, and thus he felt a need to puff himself up with the fabulous and turn his own life into fable. He couldn't hold on to a cohesive self-narrative, his words kept running away, changing from one thought into another before pooling into emotional detritus that was echoed by physical pain. No matter how much his back hurt Harry would play cricket, no matter how distorted his vision was, he refused to wear glasses and I didn't discover how badly he needed glasses for over ten years until one day when he entered looking like a horn rimmed stranger.

Now I know that Harry only ever picks up academic distinctions whether in social sciences or creative writing. In 2013 he was awarded a PhD, a two novel book deal for his novel: *The Cannibal Spirit*, which happens to have George Hunt as its protagonist, and since January 2011 he has been appointed to a university lectureship in creative writing. For years he spent sessions complaining that he could not work, and although he never came to see me dazed on his confection of recreational drugs, that was all he seemed to do at the weekends. He was in chronic pain from his damaged back, and there was the ordeal of asthma about which he will write. Codeine had become another substitute night soother. At the same time he lived in terror at the thought of being diagnosed as clinically depressed and requiring *prescribed* medication.

Harry:

> I was in therapy with Jane for thirteen years. Even as a patient, I always believed it was vital to keep a formal, professional environment of studied trust in the therapeutic space. Therapist in chair, me on couch, safely locked door, fifty-minutes-to-the-minute, a complete absence of my therapist's personal life: not the faintest whiff of countertransference to my suspicious nose. A dog barks downstairs, a son walks past on the landing, someone heard at the front door during the session: if these were understandable

as lone incidents, my rational mind shrugged even as my hackles rose in resentment at the intrusion. Is it possible to keep such formal boundaries between two people sacrosanct, for so long? Fate, chance, luck must inevitably play some role. In fact, it was precisely when immediate life intruded dramatically into the space of my therapy—those moments of more major intrusion—that proved crucial fulcrums in my evolution to the person I have become: a man built on the words and syntax I have chosen; not the confused polyphonies of other people's voices; those other people's charismatic, dominating characters with which I first arrived in therapy.

Yet the enlightening outcome of those moments of intrusion would have been impossible without a pre-existing and personal space of sympathy between Jane and I. This was born partly from the formal therapeutic trust, but was not its constituent. It was more: unique, personal, intimate—human.

Three particular intrusions stand out.

1. I am twenty-nine. A year into my therapy. Studying for my master's degree in medical anthropology. One afternoon, I stop in at the student union bar for coffee, en route to see Jane. As I am leaving, two young students push past me, laughing, cheerful daytime drunks no older than nineteen. "Fuck off!" one of them laughs at my protest. Still holding my briefcase in my left hand, I punch him hard enough to split two knuckles, and am in the process of dragging the other down the ramp to throw him in front of traffic on the Euston Road—my mind crystal cold in its planning—when the security guard who was standing at the door steps in to separate us. Twenty minutes later I arrive at Jane's, breathing short and hard with elation. Carrying a briefcase, nice, middle-class boy—but finally here to prove what I really am. She sends me to clean my hand, which is dripping celebratory blood onto her sanded floorboards. At last I have shown her what I've been trying to explain was my true character.

2. In 1999, Jane's son-in-law was killed after being attacked outside a club in Brighton. It was all over the press, and Jane inevitably was forced to tell her clients what had happened. So many of the stories of my past are wreathed in violence (as we shall see). But what can I now do, hearing her story? I stop being involved in the casual violence I have described at the student union bar. Up to that point, I had a

certain strut that my propensity to violence gave me. An identity: An identity at odds with my first class degree in anthropology, my M.Sc. with distinction. Now that strut shames me. I am tongue-tied in my sessions with Jane. I resent her not a little for forcing her private life upon me and, in doing so, taking the split syntax of my defensive dual personality from me—the boozer and fighter, and the public school boy.

3. Some two years later, and I'm standing at the very edge of the pavement beside a bus lane in Wimbledon. I've been at a football match, drinking all day, taking cocaine. I've ducked away from my friends. I'm so panicked I can no longer bear the thought of my life. I am going to topple in front of the ninety-one bus to Kingston-upon-Thames. Instead, I scramble away and huddle between two cars in a car park. I call Jane. There's just enough of faith, of trust, which tells me to make the call. Jane has drummed it into me, following similar events, though none of this intensity. "Call me," she says. "Any time. You must." It is beyond the parameters of our formalised relationship, and I have never done so before; but I have never before had the direct thought: "Kill yourself now." It scares me just more than it impels me to follow through. So I call. She is at a dinner party. A fluke she hears the phone. Some sequence of events follow: a taxi, phone numbers exchanged, Jane speaking to my mother.

There are four rooms which I have chosen as the narrative architecture of my personal history. Jane's consulting room is the first. It is the day after my near-melodrama with a bus. I lie there, reflecting, suffocated nearly with my thoughts. Then I say, "Oh God, it really is as bad as it seems." Words which are banal now. Trite even. Embarrassing. Yet they flip me into darkness. I fall down into "the foul rag and bone shop" of my heart. There I can see a foetal ball, glowing vaguely white, mucoid amid the detritus. I actually see it, the image overlying the consulting room. I howl. I cannot drive. Jane asks if she can call my mother, Coral, and for her number. She calls her. Coral collects me; drives me, in my car, home. Jane refuses to meet her.

The second room is in my room in my mother's home for seriously emotionally disturbed children—the last port of call before the secure unit. These children—abandoned by their parents, by disinterested social workers, passed through the hands of kiddy-fiddlers with foster-parenting certificates—these rejectees smash things up, drone, shriek, grope each other, sneer, flash at cars, fall out of trees, fight with tooth and nail and broken furniture, scream for hour after hour. One has flesh-fold burn marks like cooled lava flows down his back, from the kettle of boiling water mummy once poured over him. The home is lightning bolts: blasting up stairs, down long corridors and crackling in the rooms that lead off. Rain storms of grief are falling most of the time, somewhere in the house. A six year old boy is having a waking nightmare, open-eyed, staring down as his father rips out and eats his little stomach.

A short corridor leads off to a side room that is mine. I no longer share with anyone. I have my own space, being that I'm different: the owner's child. I go out each day to a public school and come back to the children's home. The room is painted dull, olive green. Its corners lie in shadow, and everywhere the lurking presence of fat house spiders. They grow as big as an adult's hand in this five hundred year old, thatched country house. Monsters patrol beneath the bed. I am lying on top (I am nine, or I am seven … am I eleven?), too afraid to reach down and turn off my electric blanket. The switch is right down between the wall and the floor is the monster's lair. The door is shut. There's some sort of screaming going on away downstairs. There's a wheeze in my lungs and it's hot. Behind the curtains above my head, a tree taps in the wind.

Breathlessness: no air goes in; nothing comes out. A fish out of its habitat: useless flapping of its mouth—open, shut. An asthma attack inhibits the functioning of your breath, stops the exhale, makes the inhale impossible. Eventually: inertia; stasis that tinges your skin slowly, surely blue. But I don't want anyone to know. Outside the room: the sniggers and the carnage, the girls' nails scratching down my face. I'm alright against the boys. I'm good at fighting. The girls are older than me, bigger than me. They are sex and violence and, as well, the whispers of malice and gossip. My mother, the children, the staff—everyone is meant to be there except me. I have no role to play. Everyone knows it.

Eventually someone always comes. "Coral-says-you-awright?" giggles a voice through the door. Or a member of staff—perhaps forgetting the room is mine—breezes in. Once: my grandmother. I'm blue, flapping and gasping. Then the syringes, the paramedics, the line of prurient faces and glowing eyes watching me being wheeled out on a stretcher even a police escort sometimes, when it's got close.

As my mother drives me home from Jane's, that dull, olive room lays itself over my vision. I see it even as I see the present: two rolls of film playing over the same screen. And I feel the emotions of both places equally: the terror of my coming apart in the present; the choking fear of what is under the bed, what is outside the door, in the past. Time is utterly delinearised. Sitting in the car, I see me lying on the bed in the children's home, my back to the door, bone-skinny heaving ribs. The city passes by, the lights refracting off the wet patches on my spectacles. I yammer and wail as my mother drives.

As I wheeze along in the ambulance, my mother sits beside me. At the children's home, I "should know better"; she "doesn't have time for this, Harry." Now, I am her "little trooper". In the hospital ward, I lie inside an oxygen tent, looking out the window at the sodium glow from the streetlamps. On the formica side table is a plastic water jug, a plastic beaker with a thermometer, fruit I won't eat in a bowl, a hardback copy of the Beano annual 1975 or 1973 or 1976. Am I eight, or six, or nine? Children murmur and thrash, but quietly. The nurse is lit by her angle-poise down the far end. My mother was here for hours. She will be back tomorrow. To stay for hours. Just her and me.

After the absence of breath; after the absence of anything in that dank, green room in the home; after all that, this softly glowing, night-time hospital ward—this third room—is the memory, even now, of my absolute and purest soothing.

When we arrive at my home from Jane's, my mother helps me upstairs. I lie on my bed in that final room: my bedroom in London. I lie there … and I lie as well on the single bed in the children's home—beside the boy I was and am. I clutch a pillow that is me. I stroke it and I feel the stroking hand on my back: my hand now, soothing me then. And, though I howl in the present, I begin to feel the peculiar attention being paid to me then, just to me, me hiding, wheezing behind the door of my room, but being soothed. I see the glow from the streetlamps in the ward around me.

At the end of the bed, not making a sound, bearing witness to the breakdown she created, my mother sits. She doesn't cry or beg to be forgiven, doesn't reject any of this, or try to help. She just bears witness. It is the most extraordinary of redemptions for us both.

When first I came to Jane, I switched between characters so often, between voices—accents, classes, my parents' words and phrases—that she could barely understand me, nor I myself. Somehow, we built a formal therapeutic space of trust. Then came the hammers to the formal mirrors of that space—my bloodied knuckles, her son-in-law's murder, my phone call to her from the point of suicide, many events of which there is no space here to tell. When those intrusions happened, when the hammer was taken to the mirrors, they proved fulcrums for my evolution. The shattering of confused syntax: the collapse of all those other people's words I was so filled with. Without the quality of the sympathy and trust between Jane and I, a quality that was what remained when mirrors came down, it could have been disastrous.

Those rooms have since become the architecture for my narrative about myself. It is a story, partly artifice, as all linearisations of the chaotic are; but it's as true as I need. And that is enough …

Harry's defence against therapeutic engagement was that he spoke in sentences that were often impossible for me to follow either intellectually or emotionally. They started full of promise and then drifted off to nowhere. I also have a tendency not to finish my sentences and enjoy using non-sequiturs. When I do this in therapy it is conscious and with the intention of leaving space for the "other" if they are feeling emotionally consonant with any developing hypothesis, to finish my sentence, or to reject it. Harry wanted to leave me isolated and panting, unable to find him amidst his syntactical hide and seek, as he writhed in his psychic pain and never happier than when he could assume the grave voice of the academe and provide me with an intriguing lecture; nothing boring, except I was bored because I thought he was seducing me into admiration.

To begin with, the only times he spoke fluently were when he was describing the failures of parenting that were inflicted by his two charismatic and *unempathic* parents, whose acts of flaunted narcissism were difficult for me to listen to. I have used the adjective unempathic, whilst protesting against its opposite empathy, which I understand as an inability for someone to recognise the impact of their acts on the emotional landscape of another person. It is in this negative emotional experience—in the absence of empathy—that I come closest to understanding why empathy is different from sympathy. Empathy is rooted in myself and not in the other. The source of its energy unlike sympathy is invisible and intuitive.

My understanding of empathy resides in the idea that we are most empathic when we achieve cumulative awareness of the impact of our words and emotions, particularly as therapists, but also critically as parents, friends, and colleagues, have upon another person's being. This feels possible and responsible to me, whereas to think I am privileged as a therapist to enter into anyone's inscape and reflect back the emotional weather feels presumptuous. There is a paradox: whilst I cannot agree to empathy being employed as a common human to human experience, I have little doubt that unempathic communication is tragically common, but one that is also affected and limited by the confines of human biology which precludes us from knowing what the other person is concealing from us, let alone thinking, or feeling, even as we sit together week after week. In instances where I have referred a patient's partner to a colleague and mutual permission has been given for the two therapists to exchange information I am often staggered by the different accounts and emphasis placed on conflicts reported, and in particular what will have been omitted by one partner and disclosed by the other.

Harry was using his mutually frustrating linguistic skills to hide from me, to hide duplicity and emotional nakedness and his global sense of shame that he was a lost boy who would never learn to "fly": as the poet MacNeice protests, "I am not yet born; O hear me" (MacNiece, 1964, p. 74). In his unfinished sentences and provocative changes of subject matter, there was deception and the impossibility of following him. Although intellectually disputed, I came to a realisation that Harry still yearned for and wanted to be found by his mother. The elusive and thorny internal imago of the distracted mother who had left him infant "hungry", still clung and left him wounded and in her thrall. *La belle dame sans merci*.

Since reading Proust—something that happened after Harry's therapy ended—I have discovered his duplicitous tactics to have a grammatical name, albeit a difficult one. It is at the heart of much of Proust's writing, as well as my own wounded psychology and also at the heart of Harry's wilful escapes from my understanding. It is a rhetorical figure of speech called "anacoluthon" which means an abrupt change in the meaning of a sentence to another sentence with a different subject, often with the intention to confuse, lose, or divert the listener.

I do not have time to talk about anacoluthon, but the word is charged with its own psychological energies, which you can choose whether or not to follow up later. I now only have time to talk about "the fifth room" in which our concluding therapy was conducted, and where the final segment of Harry's parentectomy occurred. "Who, if I cried out among the angels' hierarchy would hear me?"

I am now working in Marylebone. It is February 2007 and Harry is lying on the couch in a state of acute psychic disintegration. A splinter of me is thinking, "Oh God, why didn't we finish this therapy when things were going well, on the up, why are we back in this tortured place and what the fuck am I going to do if this gets worse, because I am not going to call his mother".

Harry's life has changed—well I thought it had—but now I am finding out that the change is superficial. He has been combining his life as a highly paid senior location manager in film with writing a novel. Highly paid but creatively unsatisfying, stressful, and physically exacting. Alongside, but neglected there is commitment to himself and to trying to write his novel but for which without the location work there is no funding and only uncertainty. There has also been the rejection of a broken engagement. Harry does not want his epitaph to be a successful negotiation with the National Trust to shoot a Nike advert. He does not want to live a life of an unbalanced material compromise. He does not want his mark in the world to be barren. Although thorns have been shed along the way, nothing emotionally stable has yet taken root. Since the broken engagement and after years of our own psychic engagement—Harry says thirteen and I say more but we are past counting—of understanding, I am his closest ally. The patient therapist dyad has all but collapsed and we now exchange books, know that we share a love of India and Tibetan art, know that we are both bible-carrying groupies of John Gray's *Straw Dogs*, which Harry first drew my attention to, and advocates of the joyous philosophy of pessimism.

Over the past months I have watched his anxiety, insomnia, and self doubt mounting to clinical proportions, I have gently suggested that his mood disorders which are almost, but yet not of bi-polar dimensions, may need *non recreational* drugs, but to Harry this suggestion, which provokes hatred and always feels like the final betrayal of his quest and a sentence to the inferno. His mother has also contributed to the idea that despite the fact that Harry is self medicating habitually, the use of anti-depressants would be a therapeutic failure.

It is almost the end of the hour, midday approaches as Harry starts to sob and writhe, he hides his eyes and curls up. Now, he is panting with terror. I know three things: I cannot abandon him at the end of the session, he does not have the money for private inpatient care and I am not going to call an ambulance and have him admitted to acute NHS psychiatric inpatient care. Although I do not know what Harry is feeling inside that foetal mess, my sympathy is palpable and although I wish it were not so, it is now accompanied by the uncomfortable sensation of pity. I know a fourth thing: I am not going to call Coral. I am not going to call his mother. I pause and try to think, there is another patient already waiting.

I call a male colleague and it is important that he is male, a general practitioner in the area. He happens to be a Parsee, I don't know if this makes any difference but I do know that his attitude is both scientific and mystical and that money will not be an issue to him in this emergency, and that Harry, like me, will respect him. I persuade his secretary to interrupt him. I explain that I am in trouble with a patient who has lost control and whose behavior is "hysterical". Yes, as the Greeks would say the "mother" is rising in him. "Mother, Mother what have you done to me" rasps Coriolanus (Shakespeare). (Father, father, where were you when your son sobbed for you?, I despair). Like a blind man I lead Harry from my consulting room, to a taxi, I cannot now remember if I get into the taxi with him, or just instruct the driver.

Harry spent the rest of that day lying intravenously sedated in a dark, spare examination room. My friend with little time to do more than keep a watchful eye; until his day's work over they talked and talked, they exchanged mobile numbers, anti-depressants were prescribed and a benign psychiatrist alerted for urgent consultation.

It took more wobbly weeks for Harry to discover that he had sprouted an inner reservoir of self hood that made it possible for him not to call out to his mother to save him, although she did pay for the psychiatrist who assessed and supervised his medication. She was as terrified as Harry. The way was lonely and the journey slow, but given time the acute anxiety abated, and Harry undertook a punishing job that required he travel alone across Southwest England location scouting for a huge television commercial almost days after this incident, with both the doctor's and my mobile numbers in his pocket, valium and anti-depressants.

Conclusion

Maturity was afoot and slowly, slowly, Harry grew up, worked out his creative priority, began to feel strong enough to risk the uncertainty of change, sat up, looked at me and thanked me, and I thanked him. In fact it was not until we ended the therapy that Harry felt strong enough to make the radical changes in his life, which led him, initially to privilege uncertainty and his creativity above spurious financial rewards. We both knew there could be no fairy tale salve to apply permanently to his wounds, although it felt like it when months later he met the young woman who has become his wife. She is also a writer, and they had ritual wedding celebrations in her homeland, Tamil Nadu. I have not met her but perhaps one day I might. Now, I like to imagine Harry becoming a father.

July 2013

I have not been in contact since Harry and myself co-authored the lecture version of the paper but now I need to send him the draft for approval. Harry replies:

> So nice to hear from you. All well my end. Nila our little daughter is wonderful, nearly eighteen-months-old, causing happy havoc. My second novel is due at publisher by 13th August (last deadline, they tell me …).

References

MacNiece, L. (1964). Prayer Before Birth. In: W. H. Auden (Ed.), *Selected Poems of Louis MacNeice*. London: Faber.

Nagy, M. (1991). *Philosophical Issues in the Psychology of C. G. Jung*. New York: State University of New York Press.

Rilke, R. M. (1981). Duino Elegies 1. In: S. Mitchell (Ed.), *The Selected Poetry of Rainer Maria Rilke*. New York: Picador.

Rilke, R. M. (2010). The First Duino Elegy. In: K. Leader, & R. Vilain (Eds.), *The Cambridge Companion to Rilke*. Cambridge: Cambridge University Press.

CHAPTER FIVE

Creating, destroying, and restoring Sanctuary within caregiving organisations: the eighteenth John Bowlby Memorial Lecture

Sandra Bloom

Introduction: changing paradigms

In the nineteenth century, an American poet named John Godfrey Saxe retold in verse, an old Indian parable about the blind men and the elephant. In the poem, six blind men travel to see what an elephant looks like and in so doing, each one individually grabs hold of a part of the elephant and mistakes it for the whole. This poem stands as a superb metaphor for our understanding of human nature up until now, with every discipline declaring its own explanations for various aspects of reality.

But a new paradigm is emerging from neuroscience, medicine, developmental paediatrics, evolutionary science, genetics, psychology, sociology, anthropology, and philosophy that is destined to change our view of human beings and our place in the world. Although still lacking an appropriate, encompassing word, this new way of thinking is already beginning to have significant impact on caregiving services under the general rubric of "trauma-informed care", because it originated in the study of post traumatic stress disorder and related complex problems.

However the study of specific reactions to traumatic experiences is only the tip of the iceberg. What is actually beginning to surface is the whole iceberg—the interconnected and fundamentally creative experience of every human being that is substantially determined by the quality and nature of early childhood attachment relationships, as Dr John Bowlby so thoroughly explored (Bowlby, 1972, 1980, 1982). Since Dr Bowlby's death, we have learned a great deal about facilitating individual growth and recovery and this chapter will briefly summarise some of the key concepts that have emerged (Bloom, 1997, 2013a). It has become evident however, that individual change should not be the only focus of intervention. Individual change is often significantly impeded by the failure of caregiving systems to change.

Unfortunately, changing systems often takes much longer than individual change, usually because groups of people tend to become stymied by the complexity of large group change and the budgets that are required to fix what is broken. It has been challenging at a practice and policy level to help people understand that we are addressing the need for what amounts to monumental change. Our minds can grasp complex concepts more quickly if we have a meaningful metaphor. Computer metaphors can be useful because just about everyone has to grapple with the challenges of these important, useful, and exceedingly frustrating devices and because now, computers are individually parts of interconnected networks. Computers have hardware and software. A wide variety of software programs can be "learned" (installed) in the computer as long as each one is compatible with the computer's "operating system"—software that allows the other software to work.

The amazing brain of a human being is constantly learning new programmes but what is the operating system for the brain? My colleagues and I think there is a sufficient body of evidence now to convince us that "attachment" is the operating system for human beings—what Dr John Bowlby, the grandfather of attachment studies, originally called the "internal working model". Exposure to trauma and other toxic forms of stress create disrupted attachment and in this metaphor, disrupted attachment can be understood as similar to a computer "virus" that wreaks havoc on the functioning of a computer. In computer networks, viruses are spread rapidly to everyone that is connected. So too do the effects of violence spread across generations and down through the generations.

At the same time we have observed that many of the staff people at every level in caregiving organisations have had experiences similar to the people they are helping. We know first-hand and have observed in virtually all varieties of human service organisations that the stress and strain of doing this work with steadily diminishing resources combined with increased regulation, loss of control, and fear of risk has taken a toll. The result is that the operating systems of our helping organisations, usually referred to as "organisational culture", have become widely dysfunctional. One of the many challenges in this work then becomes how do you purge the "virus" that has infected our systems and restore a working operating system that is upgraded, more responsive, has less bugs, crashes less, and is less vulnerable to viral attacks?

Such an upgrade requires an approach to organisational culture as a whole that is "trauma-informed" and "attachment-based", that contributes new knowledge and know-how and eliminates some of the damaged or obsolete "programming", while retaining whatever "code" is still useful and viable. The complex problems of our children cannot be fixed like you might fix a broken lamp. For them to make significant change, they need to participate in that process of change. And in the process, learn how to steer themselves into a better future. Ultimately they will have to decide what choices to make, which path in the forest will lead them out of the woods, not deeper into them.

We need to look at ways that we can rapidly shift entire treatment environments to be more effective, efficient, and speedy in helping children to change the trajectories of their lives.[1] Every caregiving organisation is a living complex adaptive system and if you want it to change, the living parts of that system must be the ones empowered to make those changes or they will not happen. Top-down change works for machines but it is not very good at all for changing children, families, or organisations. In this chapter, I will briefly describe the underpinnings of an approach to change in complex adaptive systems that is called the "Sanctuary ® Model",[2] and describe the methods we are using to transform whole cultures, creating parallel processes of recovery.

Attachment: the human operating system

Early childhood attachment determines whether a child's brain, body, sense of self, capacity for relationships, and conscience all develop properly. In our understanding of the attachment literature, we sort out seven key domains necessary for healthy growth and development. These seven domains provide the structure for the human operating system (Bloom & Farragher, 2013).[3]

Safety and security

From the moment of birth, the first responsibility of all mammalian mothers is to protect her child from harm. Every child needs the sense of safety and security provided by a stable, secure mothering relationship to use as the scaffolding for all further neuro-regulatory development.

Emotional management

The infant and early childhood relationship with mother provides the early context for emotional management. When it goes well, the mother begins the process that helps the child interact in a stable and secure way with his or her environment, using emotions to provide a basis for valuing what is worthy and unworthy in the world, ultimately informing but not dominating thought and action.

Learning

Beginning at birth, the mother must help the child learn about the world around him and how to be safe in that world, balancing learning with risk and altering the expanse of that risk as the child experiments with the world and learns from those experiments. In order for the child's cognitive abilities to unfold, the child must be protected from being overwhelmed by emotions he is not yet prepared to deal with, yet his emotional system must be stimulated enough to provoke learning.

Communication

The mother is the first great communicator for the child. In what has been described as the "serve and return" relationship between the infant and mother, the baby is learning the rudiments, the basic building blocks of communication. This flow of information back and forth must be both open so that information can come from the outside world and yet be sufficiently boundaried so that the child is not overwhelmed. The child must learn how to communicate, when to communicate, how much to communicate, and who to communicate to, and all of that will vary over time, with different people, and under differing circumstances.

Participation in relationship

Every mother must teach her child the skills necessary to survive and thrive in an increasingly interconnected and networked world. The child must learn to: listen to other people; integrate ideas and concepts; negotiate and compromise; recognise that there is no absolute truth in any situation, only the process of seeking truth. As the mother listens to the child's input, respects the child's point of view, while still asserting her own, the mother teaches the child that there are limits to one's individual strivings in interaction with others and that power is to be used, not abused.

Reciprocity and justice

In interaction with his mother, the child has his first experience with fair play. In their interaction the child begins to develop what ultimately will be a sense of justice and the basis for how just relationships are to be conducted. The child must learn how to put aside his own strivings and satisfaction of his own needs in service of "the other". If the child has experienced justice then the child will develop a concern with justice, social justice, and the common good.

Dealing with change

Within the caring scope of his mother, the child will have his first experience with loss and all of the emotional pain that accompanies loss for human beings. Every new developmental experience means learning something new and giving up something old. The child's feelings of sadness, anger, remorse, helplessness, despair will be recognised, respected, and supported by a loving mother who will provide comfort and hope that the future holds better feelings and experiences. In the process of recovering from loss, letting go and moving on in time the child will learn how to adapt, roll with life's inequities, and welcome what life holds.

Exposure to trauma, adversity, and disrupted attachment

Terminology

English is a beautiful and flexible language but there is no word that encompasses the topic of severe stress in childhood. The word "trauma" is being used as a shorthand term for what is a far more complex phenomenon. There is a stress continuum, more like the continuum that we understand goes from excellent health to terminal illness, with the constant possibility of moving back and forth on that continuum. Movement along that continuum is determined by many different factors such as the state of pre-existing health, the age of the person, the nature of the disease process, and a multitude of socio-cultural factors. Early experiences are particularly weighted because the brain is still developing and thus those experiences help to determine the way the brain gets "wired" from the very beginning, even before birth (Center on the Developing Child at Harvard University, 2010).

Similarly, in the last few decades we have learned a great deal about the continuum of stress moving from positive stress, to tolerable stress, toxic stress, traumatic stress, and all complicated by allostatic load. Stress and health interact in complex ways so that taken together exposure to stress can be seen as our number one public health problem, particularly when too much stress is experienced in childhood. All living systems deal with the stress of changing conditions and both positive and tolerable forms of stress can help us grow and develop.

Toxic stress, on the other hand, is associated with prolonged and intense activation of the body's stress response to such an extent that it can change the very architecture of a child's developing brain with problematic long-term consequences. Many factors determine the ways in which toxic stress affects a developing child—the nature of the stressor, the age of the child, the level of pre-existing health and mental health, the family situation, the number and extent of protective factors that exist within the child and the child's environment. But because human children are dependent on adult care for such an extended period of time, any experience of disrupted attachment can increase the likelihood that the child will experience toxic stress. Toxic stress exposure is being used as a way of understanding the profound effects of situations such as child physical abuse, sexual abuse, neglect, witnessing domestic violence, and being exposed to community violence, particularly when these events are repetitive, even chronic (Shonkoff, 2012; Shonkoff et al., 2012).

Traumatic stress occurs when a person experiences or witnesses an event that is overwhelming, usually life-threatening, terrifying, or horrifying in the face of helplessness. As with toxic stress exposure, the effects of traumatic stressors will be multi-determined and therefore are highly individual. The young person's pre-existing vulnerability, the nature of the stressor, the child's immediate reactions to the event or events, and what happened after the event or events, all may play a contributing role in determining the complex outcomes that the paediatrician then witnesses in practice. Traumatic events that may be experienced directly by young people include, but are not limited to, violent personal assault (sexual assault, physical attack, robbery, mugging), being kidnapped, being taken hostage, terrorist attacks, torture, incarceration, natural or human-made disasters, severe automobile accidents, or being diagnosed with a life-threatening illness. For children, sexually traumatic events may include developmentally inappropriate sexual experiences without threatened or actual violence or injury. Witnessed events include, but are not limited to, observing the serious injury or unnatural death of another person due to violent assault, accident, war, or disaster or unexpectedly witnessing a dead body or body parts. Events experienced by others that are learned about include, but are not limited to, violent personal assault, serious accident, or serious injury experienced by a family member or a close friend; learning about the sudden, unexpected death of a family member or a close friend; or learning that an attachment figure has a life-threatening disease.

Allostatic load is the term being used to describe the wear-and-tear on the body and brain that can be a result of things such as poverty, bigotry, chronic hunger, and lowered socioeconomic status. All can have a profound effect on a child's development and later health outcomes secondary to the constant stress load on the child and on his or her caregivers, even in the absence of perceivable traumatic events (Marmot, 2004; McEwen & Gianaros, 2010).

In multi-problem families, toxic stress, traumatic stress, and allostatic load factors may complexly interact, potentially creating a wide range of problems for the young people in the family. This work serves to bridge the scientific gap between long-term physiological changes, attachment theory and our growing understanding about the social determinants of health, disease and maladjustment.

Exposure to trauma, adversity and violence

In 2009, the United States Department of Justice released the findings of a comprehensive nationwide survey of the incidence and prevalence of children's exposure to violence (Finkelhor, Turner, Ormrod, Hamby & Kracke, 2009). The findings are extremely disturbing, confirming that most United States (U.S.) children are exposed to violence in their daily lives, over sixty per cent in the past year. Nearly half of the children and adolescents had been assaulted at least once in the past year. We have not even begun to reckon with the long-term public health effects of this kind of violence exposure, nor have we addressed the reality that in less than twenty years, the number of children with incarcerated parents has increased by eighty per cent (Glaze & Maruschak, 2008).

Studies of the lifespan implications of this exposure provide sobering illustrations of the long-term consequences of child maltreatment. The purpose of the adverse childhood experiences (ACE) Study done by Kaiser Permanente in San Diego and the Centers for Disease Control and Prevention in Atlanta, Georgia was to examine the impact of exposure to toxic levels of stress across the life span (Felitti & Anda, 2010). The researchers asked 18,000 willing participants—all members of the Kaiser Permanente Health Maintenance Organization in San Diego—if they would take a survey. The majority of participants were Caucasian, fifty years of age or older, and were well-educated, representing a solidly white, middle-class population.

An adversity score or ACE score was calculated by simply adding up the number of categories of exposure to a variety of childhood adversities that the person had experienced before the age of eighteen to a maximum score of ten. These categories included severe physical or emotional abuse; contact sexual abuse; severe emotional or physical neglect; living as a child with a household member who was mentally ill, imprisoned, or a substance abuser; or living with a mother who was being victimised by domestic violence; or parental separation/divorce (See: www.cdc.gov/ace/; also http://acestudy.org/; http://acesconnection.com/).

Of this largely white, middle-class, older population, almost two-thirds had an ACE score of one or more, while one in five was exposed to three or more categories of adverse childhood experience. Two-thirds of the women in the study reported at least one childhood experience involving abuse, violence, or family strife. The researchers compared the ACE score to each person's medical, mental health, and social health data and found startling and disturbing associations. The higher the ACE score, the more likely a person was to suffer from one of the following: smoking, chronic obstructive pulmonary disease, hepatitis, heart disease, fractures, diabetes, obesity, alcoholism, intravenous drug use, depression and attempted suicide, teen pregnancy, sexually transmitted diseases, poor occupational health, and poor job performance. Worse yet, the higher the ACE score, the more likely people were to have a number of these conditions interacting with each other. In other words, the higher the ACE score, the greater the impact on a person's physical, emotional, and social health.

According to the study findings, if you are a woman and have adverse childhood experiences your likelihood of being a victim of domestic violence and rape steadily increases as the ACE score rises and if you are a man, your risk of being a domestic violence perpetrator also rises. The study showed that adverse childhood experiences are surprisingly common, although typically concealed and unrecognised and that ACEs still have a profound effect fifty years later, although now transformed from psychosocial experience into organic disease, social malfunction, and mental illness.

In 2009, the results of incorporating the ACE's questions into the health surveys of five other states was released by the Centers for Disease Control indicating that fifty nine per cent of this much more diverse population had an ACE score of one or more, while nine per cent had an ACE score of five or more (Centers for Disease Control, 2010). As of 2012, at least twenty-one U.S. states are incorporating the ACE's questions into their state-wide health surveys.

A full replication of the adverse childhood experiences study—one that would take into account, for example, the other kinds of exposure that inner-city children have, in addition to the existing categories of adversity—has not yet been attempted. We do know, however, that many children who live in conditions of urban poverty are exposed to dreadful experiences. Surveys done in Detroit, Chicago, Los Angeles, and New Orleans suggest that about a quarter of young people surveyed had witnessed someone shot and/or killed during their lifetime (Bell & Jenkins, 1993; Groves, Zuckerman, Marans & Cohen, 1993; Osofsky, Wewers, Hann & Fick, 1993; Richters & Martinez, 1993). Among children at a paediatric clinic in Boston, one out of every ten children witnessed a shooting or stabbing before the age of six (Groves, Zuckerman, Marans & Cohen, 1993). Youth violence is the second leading cause of death for young people between the ages of fifteen and twenty-four in the United States. On an average day, thirteen young people are victims of homicide and almost 2,000 are treated in an emergency for injuries related to physical assault (Centers for Disease Control, 2013). In a 1998 study of 349 low-income black urban children (ages nine–fifteen), those who witnessed or were victims of violence showed symptoms of post traumatic stress disorder similar to those of soldiers coming back from war (Li, Howard, Stanton, Rachuba & Cross, 1998). The burden of violence and incarceration falls disproportionately on families of colour (Alexander, 2010; Glaze & Maruschak, 2008).

Poverty is associated with many problematic stressors that increase the likelihood that children will be exposed to both reduced opportunity and toxic stressors (Duncan, Magnuson, Boyce & Shonkoff, 2010). According to the most recent U.S. census data, one in five American children are now living below the poverty line (News, 2012).

Disrupted attachment: when things go horribly wrong

When the child has a less than optimal attachment experience as a result of exposure to trauma, adversity, neglect, and other conditions of toxic stress, the damage to the normal development of body, brain, mind, and soul can be extensive, but may have differential effects across different kinds of abilities, at different ages, in different people, even those within the same family. The people who come into any kind of caregiving setting, therefore, are likely not to have *simple* problems but instead have very complex, interrelated problems that are often related to inadequate integration of complex brain functions. Here we group these complex problems in parallel with the main attachment domains we have already articulated (Bloom & Farragher, 2013).

Lack of safety, trust, and chronic hyperarousal

Any erosion in the protective barrier that parents provide against the world can result in disrupted attachment, regardless of whether the breach in that protective envelope was intentional or not. Exposure to overwhelming events and the emotions that accompany them can change the person's central nervous system so that it takes very little stimuli to create a significant threat response—a problem called chronic hyperarousal. The loss of basic safety in early childhood has long-term consequences in the capacity to trust other people and keep oneself safe in the world.

Lack of emotional management

When a child has inadequate adult support in the face of toxic or traumatic stressors, the child is exposed to overwhelming emotions. Research has shown that toxic stress exposure has very negative consequences for normal brain and body growth and development and these effects can extend throughout adulthood. Disruptions in the capacity to manage emotional states make people much more vulnerable to a wide variety of pathological adaptations that negatively impact themselves and other people.

Learning problems

Our prolonged period of immaturity combined with high demands for complex learning means that any disruption in safety and emotional management in childhood is likely to jeopardise the unfolding of cognitive functions. Impairments in learning can be wide-ranging and far-reaching and include everything from school failure to cognitive rigidity and a failure to develop creative problem-solving skills, fully integrate disturbing elements of memory, and develop the skill-set necessary to effectively manage conflict.

Alexithymia—failure to communicate

If the child does not feel safe, cannot manage distress, and has difficulty using his cognitive capacity, then the ability to use language to communicate with others and to communicate with oneself internally is likely to be seriously impaired. The inability to give words to feelings is known as "alexithymia". We are more likely to act out in the world whatever feelings we cannot put into words and we will demonstrate through our behaviour what we are unable to convey through healthy relational communication.

Abusive power relationships

If the child does not feel safe and secure in the world, cannot adequately manage distressing emotions, cannot think well, and has difficulty openly communicating with others, then he is likely to experience increasing difficulties over time in developing the complex skills required to participate in, and resolve conflicts about, social relationships with others in school and later at work and as members of a civil society. He is likely to model power relationships based on the abusive power relationships to which he has already been exposed. This increases the likelihood that he will be bullied, bully others, or both.

Injustice and narcissism

If the child has been treated unjustly then the child's moral develop-ment will not unfold as it should. This means that the child and the adult he becomes develop a very skewed sense of right-and-wrong, ethical premises, and justice. It increases the likelihood that the child will be unable to progress to higher levels of moral functioning and instead remain preoccupied with crime and punishment, vengeance, and fulfilling his own selfish and self-gratifying needs, regardless of the consequences his behaviour may have on others.

Failure to grieve, foreshortened future

If a child has learned that the world is a dangerous place, that other people cannot be trusted, and that you can count on no one but your-self, then he is likely to resist change. All change requires loss and with-out emotional management, the emotions evoked by loss overwhelm the capacity to cope. This is dangerous when survival depends on con-stant adaptation to changing conditions. Additionally, the cognitive impairments that accompany the lack of safety and inadequate emo-tional management may also jeopardise the ability to use imagination effectively to anticipate the consequences of one's action or inaction. Lacking the ability to imagine alternatives, the person is more likely to simply repeat, to re-enact, what he already knows whether such a strategy is effective or not.

Adversity in caregiving staff

This terrible situation affects far more children—and the adults they become—than we would like to believe. Research evidence is confirm-ing what all of us in social service environments have been witnessing first hand—that exposure to toxic stress is epidemic. Most people in the United States will experience a traumatic event at some time in their lives.

People who have experienced the impact of toxic stress as children do not just "leave it at the door" when they enter the workplace. In our own informal surveys and one formal survey of people working in health care, social services, education, and mental health service deliv-ery for children and for adults we have found that most of the staff members we surveyed had suffered some kind of serious childhood adversity (Esaki & Larkin, 2013). Recognising this reality, the National Academy of Science has asserted that a growing proportion of the U.S. workforce in the future will have diminished cognitive and social skills secondary to being raised in disadvantaged environments (Knudsen, Heckman, Cameron & Shonkoff, 2006).

And then there is the danger that is present, even at work. Since the 1980s, violence has been recognised as a leading cause of occupational mortality and morbidity. On average, 1.7 million workers are injured each year (about half of these injuries occur in health care and social services), and more than 800 die as a result of workplace violence (NIOSH, 2006). After law enforcement, people working in the mental health sector in the United States are the most likely to be victimised while at work (Bloom & Farragher, 2010).

National reports declare that at present and in the foreseeable future, the social services are experiencing a workforce crisis (Hoge et al., 2007). This crisis is evident in high turnover rates in many social service organisations—sometimes as high as fifty per cent. If we want to keep good workers and attract more, then we must create organisations within which their deficits are minimised and their strengths maximised. We do not believe that our present human service delivery environments can measure up to those expectations.

Trauma-organised systems

People who have a history of exposure to adversity, toxic stress, and trauma have complex problems and are challenging to all health and human service delivery environments (Bloom, 2011; Bloom & Farragher, 2010, 2013). At the same time, the people who work in these organisations may have experienced traumatic events themselves and many will have experienced adversity as children. And the organisation as a whole often has in its history some terrible events that have occurred. It is impossible to understand the full impact of the last thirty years of changes in human service delivery without understanding the impact of acute and chronic stress on workers at every level of the system.

In most human service delivery organisations, workload and job complexity have increased while financial incentives have decreased. Because of decreased funding, many organisations hire fewer people with advanced training and experience, depending more on a non-professional, often unskilled and inexperienced workforce to provide twenty-four-hour-a-day care for the most injured people in our culture. The higher the turnover rate, the more of a problem this is. Budgets for education, training, supervision, case review have all declined while the regulatory demands of federal, state, local, and managed care organisations have skyrocketed. Rampant programme closures have put extreme pressure on existing organisations to cope with the demands for service, while insurance company constraints require increasingly rapid turnover of clients.

We believe that organisations—including human service organisations are, like individuals, complex, adaptive, living systems (Pascale, Millemann & Gioja, 2000). Being alive, they are vulnerable to stress, particularly chronic and repetitive stress. Chronic stress stealthily robs an organisation of basic interpersonal safety and trust and thereby robs an organisation of health. Organisations, like individuals, can be traumatised and the result of traumatic experience can be as devastating for organisations as it is for individuals. As a result, many human service delivery networks are functioning as "trauma-organised systems" (Bentovim, 1992).

Parallel process

Since organisations are living complex systems and as such are vulnerable to the impact of trauma and chronic stress, we suggest that as a result of acute and chronic organisational stress, destructive processes occur within and between organisations that mirror or "parallel" the processes for which our clients seek help. In an organisational context, parallel process can be defined as what happens when "two or more systems—whether these consist of individuals, groups, or organisations—have significant relationships with one another, they tend to develop similar affects, cognition, and behaviours, which are defined as parallel processes. Parallel processes can be set in motion in many ways, and once initiated leave no one immune from their influence" (Smith, Simmons & Thames, 1989, p. 13).

The result of these complex interactions between traumatised clients, stressed staff, pressured organisations, and a social and economic environment that is frequently hostile to the aims of recovery is often the opposite of what was intended. Staff in many treatment programs suffer physical and psychological injuries at alarming rates and thus become demoralised and hostile. Their counter-aggressive responses to the aggression in their clients help to create punitive environments. Leaders become variously perplexed, overwhelmed, ineffective, authoritarian, or avoidant as they struggle to satisfy the demands of their superiors, to control their subordinates, and to protect their clients. When professional staff and non-professionally trained staff gather together in an attempt to formulate an approach to complex problems they are not on the same page. They lack a common theoretical framework that informs problem-solving. Without a shared way of understanding the problem, what passes as treatment may be little more than labelling, the prescription of medication, and behavioural "management." When troubled clients fail to respond to these measures, they are labelled again, given more diagnoses and termed "resistant to treatment." In this way, our systems inadvertently but frequently recapitulate the very experiences that have proven to be so toxic for the people we are supposed to help.

Destroying Sanctuary

Just as the lives of people exposed to repetitive and chronic trauma, abuse, and maltreatment become organised around the traumatic experience, so too can entire systems become organised around the recurrent and severe stress of trying to cope with a flawed mental model based on individual pathology that is the present underpinning of our helping systems. When this happens, it sets up an interactive dynamic that creates what are sometimes uncannily parallel processes (Bloom & Farragher, 2010). Focusing on the seven domains we have explored above, let's look at how these parallel processes appear in an organisational context.

Lack of safety, trust, and crisis driven

The human service system and virtually every component of it, including the mental health system, have been and continue to be under conditions of chronic stress, individually and collectively experiencing repetitive trauma. In many helping organisations, neither the staff nor the administrators feel particularly safe with their clients or even with each other. Acute crisis often leads to chronic states of organisational crisis and organisational hyperarousal. This lack of safety may present as a lack of physical safety, workplace violence, abusive behaviour on the part of managers and/or staff, and a pervasive mistrust of the organisation. A perceived lack of safety erodes trust, which is the basis for positive social relationships. As a result these organisations are very tightly wrapped and tensions run high. Under such unrelenting stress, helping professionals and the agencies themselves become more highly reactive and are more ready to see threat rather than opportunity, pathology rather than strength, and risk rather than reward. The protection that we provide for each other in groups—our "social immunity" becomes eroded under conditions of chronic crisis and unrelenting stress and no one feels safe.

Loss of emotional management

A core challenge for clients served by human services is the ability to manage distressing emotions, while at the same time being able to extend empathy to their clients and not become emotionally anesthetised. Emotional intelligence is recognised as an important component of any workplace environment that hopes to be productive and healthy. But emotional intelligence is slow to develop or eroded when fear, recurrent crisis, unrelenting stress, and unmanaged conflict come to dominate a work environment. Emotions are contagious and under any conditions, human service delivery environments demand the highest levels of emotional labour from workers. Stress and trauma exacerbate those demands. Atmospheres of recurrent or constant crisis severely constrain the ability of staff to manage their own emotions, and this makes it difficult to provide healing environments for their clients and in this way contribute to poor services. Negative emotions become collective emotions. Under these circumstances, conflict escalates and both relationships and problem-solving suffer.

Organisational learning disabilities, dissociation, and amnesia

Under the conditions we have been describing, stress interferes with organisational learning, organisational memory is lost, organisational amnesia affects function, and service delivery becomes increasingly fragmented and dissociated. Decision making becomes compromised and reactive so that short-sighted policy decisions are made that appear to compound existing problems. Dissent is silenced, leading to simplification of decisions and lowered morale. The organisation becomes progressively learning disabled and this severely compromises its capacity to adapt to changing conditions.

Organisational miscommunication, conflict, and alexithymia

Human communication in groups is always challenging. The discoveries we made as children about how easily a message can become garbled as it is transmitted one-by-one through a group are just as relevant to adult workplaces, complicated even further by the elimination of nonverbal information via email and texting. Under conditions of chronic stress, breakdowns in organisational communication networks occur. The feedback loops that are necessary for consistent and timely error correction no longer function. Without adequate networks of communication, the normal conflict that exists in human groups will escalate and increasing amounts of important information becomes "undiscussable"—arising as the "elephants" in the organisational room. As a result the organisation as a whole becomes increasingly alexithymic, unable to talk about the issues that are causing the most problems and that remain, therefore, unsolvable. Without the ability to discuss vital subjects, the organisational grapevine becomes poisoned, conflict compounds, and without adequate communication, collective disturbances emerge that, if not stopped, will lead to chronic unresolved conflict and violence.

Authoritarianism, learned helplessness, silenced dissent

Rarely does the subject of power—who has it, who doesn't, and how it is used and abused—come up for open discussion in social service environments and yet it is a critical component of any organisational setting. As communication breaks down, errors compound, and the situation feels increasingly out of control, organisational leaders become more controlling and authoritarian. Under these circumstances, workplace bullying is likely to increase at all levels, and organisations may become vulnerable to petty tyrants. As the organisation becomes more hierarchical and autocratic, there is a progressive and simultaneous isolation of leaders and a "dumbing down" of staff, with an accompanying "learned helplessness" and loss of critical thinking skills. The organisation and the individuals in it become highly risk avoidant. Efforts to empower workers may pay only lip service to true participatory processes resulting in what amounts to bogus empowerment. Dissent is unwelcome in environments characterised by chronic stress because dissent is seen as a threat to unified action. As a result the quality of problem analysis and decision making deteriorates further. Because dissent serves as corrective feedback within an organisation thus averting disaster, the silencing of dissent is dangerous to organisational and individual well-being.

Punishment, revenge, and organisational injustice

The notion that "punishment works" is simply taken for granted as true, as part of our existing mental model for dealing with other people. An abundance of scientific research shows that the utility of punishment is largely a myth. But as leaders become more stressed they become more authoritarian, controlling, and coercive. When these efforts to correct problems are ineffective, organisational stress increases further. Under these conditions, punitive measures are likely to be employed in an effort to control workers and clients. Organisational practices that are perceived as unjust evoke a desire for vengeance. Human beings who believe they have been punished unfairly quite naturally seek revenge in their interpersonal relationships and in the workplace and this response can produce more injustice as well as workplace sabotage. As in the case of the chronically stressed individual, shame, guilt, anger, and a desire for justice can combine with unfortunate consequences. When this is happening, the organisation may become both socially irresponsible and ethically compromised and otherwise decent people may stand around and do nothing to intervene.

Unresolved grief, re-enactment, and decline

Because the existing mental model for organisations is based on notions of rationality, control, and social engineering, the human reactions to loss of attachments is given little recognition. Nonetheless, loss, grief, and traumatic loss have become commonplace components of human service environments. Staff, leaders, and programs depart. Neighbouring systems close. Standards of care deteriorate and quality assurance standards are lowered in an attempt to deny or hide this deterioration. Over time, leaders and staff lose sight of the essential purpose of their work together and derive less and less satisfaction and meaning from the work. People begin to question whether they are actually successful at what they do or just permanently failing. When this is occurring, staff members feel increasingly angry, demoralised, helpless, and hopeless about the people they are working to serve: they become "burned out." Unresolved loss increases the tendency of human beings to repeat the past and re-enact tragedy and loss. All change involves loss, but without an ability to acknowledge, honour, and work through repetitive loss, organisations are likely to develop ever-increasing problems and a powerful tendency to repeat ineffective strategies. This re-enactment behaviour can ultimately lead to decline and even organisational death. Most disturbing is the idea that the broader society may unconsciously set up the social service sector to actually be successful failures (Seibel, 1999).

The Sanctuary Model

The four pillars of Sanctuary

"Creating Sanctuary" refers to the shared experience of creating and maintaining physical, psychological, social, and moral safety within a social environment—any social environment—and thus reducing systemic violence (Bloom, 1997, 2013a, 2013b, 2013c; Bloom & Farragher, 2013; Esaki et al., 2013). As it became clear that the process of "creating Sanctuary" had to aim at organisational culture we realised that there are key aspects of changing culture and creating community. There has to be a shared knowledge base, shared values, shared language, and shared practice. We call these the four pillars of Sanctuary.

Our shared knowledge comprises our present knowledge about trauma, toxic stress, adversity, attachment, and recovery. Trauma-informed, attachment-based organisational change requires radical alterations in the basic mental models upon which thought and action are based and without such change, treatment is bound to fall unnecessarily short of full recovery or fail entirely. This change in mental models must occur on the part of the clients, their families, the staff, and the leaders of the organisation. Mental models exist at the level of very basic assumptions, far below conscious awareness and everyday function and yet they guide and determine what we can and cannot think about and act upon (Bloom & Farragher, 2013; Senge, 1994).

The seven commitments of Sanctuary are a value system tied directly to trauma-informed treatment goals. S.E.L.F. provides us with a shared language and organising framework. The Sanctuary toolkit then offers practical skill-building that reinforces and strengthens individual and group commitment to change. The process of "creating Sanctuary" begins with getting everyone on the same page—surfacing, sharing, arguing about, and finally agreeing on the basic values, beliefs, guiding principles, and philosophical principles that are to guide attitudes, decisions, problem-solving, conflict resolution, and behaviour. Out of this process our shared mission emerges: creating and sustaining a parallel process of recovery for clients, families, staff members, organisations, and even societies.

The Sanctuary Commitments

The Sanctuary Model is structured around a philosophy of belief and practice that creates a process enabling organisations to shift their mental models. For a complex organisation to function you need just the right number of principles that guide short-term, everyday conduct as well as long-term strategy. Too many rules and a system becomes rigid, inflexible, and even paralysed. Too few and it becomes purely individualistic and chaotic. The Sanctuary Commitments structure the organisational norms that determine the organisational culture. The Sanctuary Commitments represent the guiding principles for implementation of the Sanctuary Model—the basic structural elements of the Sanctuary "operating system"—and each commitment supports trauma recovery goals for clients, families, staff, and the organisation as a whole.

We didn't invent these principles. Other than the newer scientific findings around toxic stress, trauma, and attachment, these commitments represent universal principles, ancient wisdom that is as old as human groups. We have simply compiled them, articulated them into a cohesive whole, and developed a methodology to get disparate groups organised around them. And they cannot be "cherry-picked". All seven Sanctuary Commitments are complexly interactive and interdependent. Take away one and the whole structure may fall apart.

The Sanctuary Commitments apply to everyone. Organisational leaders must be fully committed to the process of the Sanctuary Model for it to be effective—that means the board of directors, managers at all levels, and every person who works in the organisation. If the organisational leaders do not get on-board, it will not work. At first glance, many organisational leaders hear a review of the seven commitments and believe that those commitments already constitute their organisational culture. In many cases this is at least partially true. It is only when leaders engage in a different kind of dialogue with other members of their organisational community that they find out how divergent people's views are on what these commitments mean and how to make them real in everyday interactions. Experience has taught that courageous leadership is critical to system change and without it, substantial change is unlikely to occur. In the following sections we will briefly describe the Sanctuary Commitments as they run in parallel with the individual and organisational domains (Bloom & Farragher, 2013).

Commitment to Nonviolence

The Commitment to Nonviolence refers to the active creation of non-violent environments important not just because our caregiving environments have become dangerous and unsafe for the people who work in them and who seek help. It is because we must learn—as a whole species—how to practice nonviolence in our daily lives, everywhere, all of the time. Institutions then—hospitals, mental health programs, group homes, prisons, shelters, schools—become laboratories for what is required if life is to survive—a social revolution. Working and living non-violently takes tremendous discipline, self-reflection, and group support. Many of the components of the Sanctuary Toolkit, like community meetings and safety plans are designed to facilitate nonviolent action.

Commitment to Emotional Intelligence

Emotional intelligence refers to the ability to identify, understand and put into words one's own feelings, to accurately read and comprehend emotional states in others, to manage strong emotions and to express them in a constructive manner, to regulate one's own behaviour, to develop empathy for others and to establish and sustain relationships. Since this is a primary problem in all of our institutions, the development of emotional management skills is a primary function. To do that organisations must build respect for the tough emotional labour that all staff members engage in, minimise the paralysing effects of fear, and expand awareness of problematic cognitive-behaviour patterns and how to change them—in everyone.

Commitment to Social Learning

The Commitment to Social Learning is a whole organisational culture vow to create a "living-learning" environment for clients, their families, and everyone that works in the setting (Jones, 1968). An underlying assumption in this is that we are in the market of positive change, that if people are exactly the same (or worse) after leaving our care, then we have done a terrible job. The Sanctuary Model is not about stabilisation. We believe that everybody can change, even if it is just a little bit. But change that is self-determined has to come about by learning something. We learn things in the context of relationship. So we believe that the Sanctuary Model has to guide an organisation in creating an environment where everyone within that institution has multiple opportunities to learn, grow, adapt, and change in a way that benefits them and their society. That means we must all unlearn some things, learn some new things, remember useful information from the past, and let go of things from the past that are no longer useful. It requires us to develop better decision-making and problem solving capacities, part of which is learning to honour dissent.

Commitment to Open Communication

In an organisation, the communication network is an analogue to the vascular system of our bodies. Any breakdown in that system causes dysfunction and potentially, death. The goal of this commitment is to help organisational members overcome barriers to healthy communication. There are many barriers today from the overuse of electronic communication, to the lack of productive meetings and to the absence of meaningful dialogue. To overcome these barriers, people will have to dare to discuss the "undiscussables"—the important things that are talked about only in the meetings-after-the-meetings (Hammond & Mayfield, 2004). Only by doing so can they overcome the organisational alexithymia—the inability to put into words the most disturbing aspects of organisational function. This means increasing transparency, developing better conflict management skills, and establishing or reinforcing healthy boundaries.

Commitment to Democracy

This is the commitment that is the most misconstrued and the least understood, largely because our understanding of what democracy is has become so watered down, unpractised, and marginalised that most people seem to think it just means voting. In the Sanctuary Model, the Commitment to Democracy means much more than that. The definition we use is that democracy "represents the ideal of a cohesive community of people living and working together and finding fair, nonviolent ways to reconcile conflicts" (Gastil, 1993, p. 5). The Commitment to Democracy is really about how we deal with the issue of power and its abuse in our organisations accompanied by a recognition that people support what they help to create and if they don't help to create it they are not likely to support it. It fully recognises that the problems we face are collective and that the only good solutions will also be collective. In order to get to those solutions—regardless of whether we are talking about a child in residential care or the state of our global climate—we are talking about the need for emergent solutions and those have to emerge from the brains of people who know how to get along together, how to civilly disagree with each other, how to compromise, bargain, negotiate, and synthesise. Along with the Commitment to Nonviolence, creating participatory environments is fundamental to any real and lasting change within our human service delivery environments.

Commitment to Social Responsibility

Social responsibility is a notion that has become almost passé in our fiercely competitive, market-driven, consumer culture. But human nature hasn't changed and we are deeply programmed for justice for ourselves and social justice for each other. In the Sanctuary Model, this commitment urges us to harness the energy of reciprocity and a yearning for justice by rebuilding restorative social connection skills, establishing healthy and fair attachment relationships, and transforming the desire for revenge into a driving need for social justice and concern for the common good.

Commitment to Growth and Change

This final commitment focuses on two significant domains: loss and change. An unavoidable fact of life is that all growth, all change necessitates loss. In fact, we usually have to give something up before we get the rewards of something new. Our experience tells us that the fundamental sign of a failure to finish the grieving process is repeating the past or "re-enactment". That means that an organisation that hopes to be productive, useful, and healthy for all organisational members must face this fundamental fact and cease repeating irrelevant or destructive past patterns of thought, feeling, and behaviour. Human beings avoid pain and we will not let go of old habits—comforting because they are predictable—unless we have a vision of a possible future that we want to get to, worth the risk of letting go to see what happens next.

S.E.L.F.

What we have just described is a value system, relatively easy to agree with, *really* difficult to practice consistently—that's why we call them "commitments"—it's what we want to do in our hearts, even if sometimes our actions fall short. The better we get at it, however, the fewer messes we have to clean up. Nonetheless, it's complicated and S.E.L.F. makes it a bit more manageable on a practical level.

S.E.L.F. is an acronym that represents the four key interdependent aspects of recovery from bad experiences. S.E.L.F. provides a nonlinear, cognitive-behavioural, psychoeducational approach for facilitating movement through the Sanctuary Commitments—regardless of whether we are talking about individual client, family, or staff problems, or whole organisational dilemmas. It is a framework that helps to organise what are often chaotic amounts of information and as a result imposes a sense of coherence upon that information, making it more comprehensible, manageable, and meaningful (Antonovsky, 1987).

S.E.L.F. is a compass that allows us to explore all four key domains of healing, all of the time. As the importance of one or another of these domains shifts over time, sometimes within minutes, the interpersonal dialogue can shift as well and just as rapidly. *Safety* is about attaining safety—physical, psychological, social, and moral safety—within oneself, in relationships, and in a variety of different environments. *Emotional management* focuses on identifying levels of various emotions and developing skills to modulate emotion in response to memories, persons, or events in a way that fosters safety to self and others. *Loss* addresses feelings of grief in dealing with personal losses and recognising that all change involves loss, that working through loss is a process, and that letting go can be facilitated by the support of others. *Future* is about "the vision thing" and encourages people to try out new roles, ways of relating and behaving as a "survivor" to ensure personal safety, envisioning a different and better future. We believe that the energy for change actually resides in the future and is always there to be drawn upon as a motivating force.

Using S.E.L.F., the clients, their families, and staff are able to embrace a shared, non-technical and non-pejorative language that allows them all to see the larger recovery process in perspective. The accessible language demystifies what sometimes is seen as confusing and even insulting clinical or psychological terminology that can confound clients and staff, while still focusing on the aspects of pathological adjustment that pose the greatest problems for everyone.

Sanctuary Toolkit

The Sanctuary Toolkit comprises a range of practical skills that enable individuals and groups to more effectively and consistently use the Sanctuary Commitments in daily practice, build a sense of community and develop a deeper and more comprehensive understanding about the effects of trauma and adversity while gaining the ability to respond to those effects in a positive way.

The Sanctuary Institute

The Sanctuary Institute is a five-day intensive training experience.[4] Teams of five to eight people, from various levels of the organisation, come together to learn from our faculty, who are colleagues from other organisations implementing Sanctuary. Together teams begin to create a shared vision of the kind of organisation they want to create. These teams will eventually become the Sanctuary steering committee for their organisation. The training experience usually involves several organisations at the same time and generally these organisations are very different in terms of size, scope, region, and mission. This diversity helps to provide a rich learning experience for the participants.

During the training, the steering committee engages in prolonged facilitated dialogue that serves to surface the major strengths, vulnerabilities, and conflicts within the organisation. By looking at shared assumptions, goals, and existing practice, staff members from various levels of the organisation are required to share in an analysis of their own structure and functioning, often asking themselves and each other provocative questions that have never been overtly surfaced before. Many of these questions have not been raised before because participants have never felt safe enough to say what has been on their mind or in their hearts, even after many years of working together. Although the continual focus is on the fundamental question of: "Are we safe?", participants quickly learn that in the Sanctuary Model being safe means being willing to take risks by being willing to say what needs to be said and hear what needs to be heard.

Participants look at the change process itself and are asked to anticipate the inevitable resistance to change that is a fact of life in every organisation. They look at management styles, the way decisions are made and conflicts resolved. In the process of these discussions, they learn about what it means to engage in more democratic processes on the part of leaders, staff, and clients in terms of the simultaneous increase in rights and responsibilities. They evaluate the existing policies and procedures that apply to staff, clients, and families and ask whether or not they are effective in achieving their shared goals. They are asked to learn about and become thoroughly familiar with the psychobiology of trauma and disrupted attachment and the multiple ways that post traumatic stress in all of its manifestations are present in the lives of the children, adults and families they work with. They are challenged to begin thinking about the implications of that knowledge for treatment. They also learn how high levels of stress in the organisation can impact relationships, emotions, and decision making at every level of the organisation. They develop an understanding of the conceptual tool for organising treatment that we refer to as "S.E.L.F.". They learn about vicarious trauma, traumatic re-enactment, and the importance of understanding themselves and providing support for each other. And they are introduced to the various components of the Sanctuary Toolkit including community meetings, safety plans, red flag reviews, S.E.L.F. psychoeducation, S.E.L.F. treatment planning, and Sanctuary team meetings.

Participants report that the week-long training is a powerful experience—some have said even life-changing. It needs to be because they have a big job to go home to. They will need to go back to their respective organisations and begin to change the culture of the organisation and change long standing paradigms and patterns of behaviour.

Developing a core team and guided implementation manuals

The Sanctuary steering committee is instructed to go back to their organisation and create a "core team"—a larger, multidisciplinary team that expands its reach into the entire organisation. It is this core team that will be the activators of the entire system. The core team should have representatives from every level of the organisation to insure that every "voice" is heard. It is vital that all key organisational leaders become actively involved in the process of change and participate in this core team. The core team is armed with a Sanctuary direct care staff training manual, a Sanctuary indirect staff training manual, a Sanctuary implementation manual, several psychoeducational curricula, and on-going consultation and technical assistance from Sanctuary faculty members to guide them through the process of Sanctuary implementation that extends over three years and hopefully leads to Sanctuary certification.

Organisational change takes several years to really get traction and then continues—hopefully—forever. The objective of the implementation and technical assistance is to edge an organisation closer and closer to the "edge of chaos" where creative, self-organising change occurs, without destabilising it to such a point that it becomes chaotic and dangerous. As the former C.E.O. of Andrus Children's Center, Nancy Ment, has noted, "The Sanctuary Model doesn't keep bad things from happening but it allows an organisation to deal with those bad things without losing its way so it can bounce back and continue to function" (In a conversation, 2011).

The responsibility of core team members is to actively represent and communicate with their constituents and to become trainers and cheerleaders for the entire organisation. The core team works out team guidelines and expectations of involvement for individual team members as well as a meeting schedule and decide on safety rules for the constructive operation of the team itself. The core team is ultimately responsible for the development of an implementation process aimed at including the entire organisation in the change process that involves teaching everyone about the Sanctuary Commitments, attachment theory, trauma theory, S.E.L.F., and the Sanctuary Toolkit. The core team facilitates the development of educational programs for direct care staff as well as indirect care staff who work in human resource, finance, facilities management, food service, and administration. It is likely that the core team will facilitate changes in admissions, interviewing of new staff, orientation programmes, supervision, as well as training and education policies. They oversee a plan for significantly greater client participation in planning and implementation of their own service plan and figure out how they are going to engage a wider network of their stakeholders in the Sanctuary change process. The ultimate goal is to take meaningful steps to change the organisation's culture and engage as many community members as possible in that process.

As discussions begin in the core team, participating staff begin to make small but significant changes. Members take risks with each other and try new methods of engagement and conflict resolution. They feed these innovations and their results, back into the process discussions. The core team must always maintain a balance between process and product. It is not enough to talk about how we will change things. We must also make actual changes in the way we do business. The core team therefore not only plans together how best to share what they are learning with the larger organisation, and trains all agency personnel and clients in the Sanctuary principles, but also decides how to integrate the Sanctuary Toolkit into the day-to-day operation of the organisation and how to evaluate how these initiatives are taking hold in the organisation.

Through the implementation steps of the Sanctuary Model, staff members engage in prolonged dialogue that serves to surface the major strengths, vulnerabilities, and conflicts within the organisation. By looking at shared assumptions, goals, and existing practice, staff members from various levels of the organisation are required to share in an analysis of their own structure and functioning, often asking themselves and each other provocative questions that have never been overtly surfaced before. As this happens, the development of more democratic, participatory processes begin to emerge. These processes are critical because they are most likely to lend themselves to the solution of very complex problems while improving staff morale, providing checks and balances to abuses of power, and opening up the community to new sources of information.

Evaluation and expected outcomes

Finally, the core team must decide on indicators they want to use to evaluate their Sanctuary program in an on-going way—their Sanctuary program evaluation plan. The indicators should be observable and measurable and consistent with standards established by Sanctuary leaders. There should be a regular process of evaluation and review that involves all core team members. It is vital that there be a thorough method for reviewing problems and failures and establishing remedial courses of action. But likewise there must be methods for reviewing and capturing successes.

The impact of creating a trauma-informed, Sanctuary Model culture should be observable and measurable. The outcomes we expect to see include and are applicable to all community members: less violence including physical, verbal, emotional forms of violence, including but not limited to reduced/eliminated seclusion and restraint; system-wide understanding of complex biopsychosocial and developmental impact of trauma and abuse and what that means for the service environment; less victim-blaming; less punitive and judgmental responses; clearer more consistent boundaries, higher expectations, linked rights and responsibilities; earlier identification of and confrontation with abusive use of power in all of its forms; better ability to articulate goals, create strategies for change, justify need for holistic approach; understanding and awareness of re-enactment behaviour, resistance to change and how to achieve a different outcome; more democratic environment at all levels; more diversified leadership and embedding of leadership skills in all staff; better outcomes for children, staff, and organisation.

The Sanctuary Network

Our belief in the power of community led us to develop the Sanctuary Institute. The Sanctuary Institute is the gateway to the Sanctuary Network a community of organisations committed to the development of trauma-informed services. We are all committed to the belief that we can do better for our clients and our colleagues as well as our society if we can accept that the people we serve are not sick or bad, but injured and that the services we provide must provide hope, promote growth and inspire change.

At the present time over two hundred and fifty human service delivery programmes from around the United States and internationally are working through the implementation process. A number of programs have become Sanctuary-certified. They include adult inpatient psychiatric and substance abuse facilities, domestic violence shelters, residential programs and group homes for children, schools and educational programs, juvenile justice facilities, and a number of large programs that have a wide variety of inpatient, outpatient, partial, and residential programs. The Sanctuary Model is still evolving, and we remain engaged in the process of co-creation with other members of the Sanctuary Network.

Sanctuary certification and research

Sanctuary is a registered trademark and the right to use the Sanctuary name is contingent on engagement in the Sanctuary Institute training and certification program and an agreement to participate in an on-going, multi-year, peer-review certification process. Programs usually seek Sanctuary certification in the two to three year period after participation in the Sanctuary Institute. Research is underway in the hope of moving the Sanctuary Model from an "evidence-supported" to an "evidence-based" approach. In this way we hope to establish a method for guaranteeing an acceptable level of fidelity to the original model upon which the research was based (Bloom, 2013b; Esaki et al., 2013; Rivard et al., 2003; Rivard, Bloom, McCorkle & Abramovitz, 2005; Rivard et al., 2004).

Summary

We believe that the current operating system for the human service delivery system is outdated, mechanistic, and inappropriate to human health and well-being. This helps to explain why there are so many chronic clashes between our organisations and the living individuals who entirely comprise them. In order to adequately address the needs of the traumatised clients who fill the ranks of our trauma-organised human service delivery system, we need a new operating system— what is being referred to now as a "trauma-informed" operating system—for human service delivery organisations. Just as attachment is the basis of the individual operating system, social relationships are the basis of organisational functioning as well. We believe that in a parallel way, traumatic experience and adversity can profoundly disrupt the operating systems of organisations. We believe that the current mechanistic model of organisational functioning is a result of destructive and potentially lethal parallel processes secondary to chronic stress that have created a seriously flawed operating system for human service organisations and entire systems. The Sanctuary Model represents an evidence-supported, attachment-based, trauma-informed, theoretical, and practical approach to changing organisational cultures so that human service delivery organisations serving children, adults, and families can be healthier, safer places to work and to heal.

Notes

1. The reader will note a switch in this document from single to plural, from the "I" to the "we". This is because the knowledge I am writing about as a singular author has been derived largely from complex, long-lasting group processes that can only be reflected in this way. In the previous pages, for the sake of brevity, I refer to the mothering person as a "she" and the child as a "he", knowing full well that half of the children in the world are "she-s" and some of the mothering people are "he-s". I wish we would find some grammatically new words that are more gender neutral but I do not like calling child an "it". I apologise in advance for any unintended offence.
2. For more information about the Sanctuary Model, see www.sanctuaryweb.com as well as Bloom and Farragher (2013).
3. For an up-to-date review of critical work in the field of attachment studies and exposure to adversity go to Center on the Developing Child, Harvard University at http://developingchild.harvard.edu/
4. The Sanctuary Institute (www.thesanctuaryinstitute.org) is a part of the Andrus Children's Center in Yonkers, NY. www.andruschildren.org. For more information contact Sarah Yanosy, Director, 914-965-2700 x1117 or syanosy@jdam.org.

References

Alexander, M. (2010). The New Jim Crow: Mass Incarceration in the Age of Colorblindness. New York: The New Press.

Antonovsky, A. (1987). Unraveling the Mystery of Health: How People Manage Stress and Stay Well. San Francisco: Jossey Bass.

Bell, C., & Jenkins, E. (1993). Community violence and children on Chicago's southside. *Psychiatry, 56*: 46–54.

Bentovim, A. (1992). *Trauma-Organized Systems: Physical and Sexual Abuse in Families*. London: Karnac Books.

Bloom, S. L. (1997). Creating Sanctuary: Toward the Evolution of Sane Societies. New York: Routledge.

Bloom, S. L. (2011). Trauma-organized systems and parallel process. In: N. Tehrani (Ed.), *Managing Trauma in the Workplace: Supporting Workers and Organizations*, (pp. 139–153). London: Routledge.

Bloom, S. L. (2013a). *Creating Sanctuary: Toward the Evolution of Sane Societies*, (2nd edition). New York: Routledge.

Bloom, S. L. (2013b). The Sanctuary model: Changing habits and transforming the organizational operating system. In: J. D. Ford, & C. A. Courtois (Eds.), *Treating Complex Traumatic Stress Disorders in Childhood and Adolescence*. New York: Guilford Press.

Bloom, S. L. (2013c). The Sanctuary Model: Rebooting the organizational operating system in group care setting. In: R. Reece, C. Hanson, & J. Sargeant (Eds.), *Treatment of Child Abuse: Common Ground for Mental Health, Medical, and Legal Practitioners*. Baltimore, MD: John Hopkins University Press.

Bloom, S. L., & Farragher, B. (2010). *Destroying Sanctuary: The Crisis in Human Service Delivery Systems*. New York: Oxford University Press.

Bloom, S. L., & Farragher, B. (2013). Restoring Sanctuary: A New Operating System for Trauma-Informed Systems of Care. New York: Oxford University Press.

Bowlby, J. (1972). *Attachment and Loss, Volume II. Separation*. New York: Basic Books.

Bowlby, J. (1980). *Attachment and Loss, Volume III: Loss, Sadness and Depression*. New York: Basic Books.

Bowlby, J. (1982). *Attachment and Loss, Volume I. Attachment*. New York: Basic Books.

Center on the Developing Child at Harvard University. (2010). The foundations of lifelong health are built in early childhood. National forum on early childhood policy and programs. Available at: www.developingchild.harvard.edu. Accessed July 8, 2012.

Centers for Disease Control. (2010). Adverse Childhood Experiences Reported by Adults—Five States, 2009. *Mortality and Morbidity Review, 59(49)*: 1609–1613.

Centers for Disease Control. (2013). 2012 Youth violence fact sheet. Available at: www.cdc.gov/violenceprevention/youthviolence/. Accessed December 29, 2013.

Duncan, G., Magnuson, K., Boyce, T. A., & Shonkoff, J. (2010). The long reach of early childhood poverty: Pathways and impacts. Cambridge, MA: Center for the Developing Child, Harvard University. Available at: http://developingchild.harvard.edu/initiatives/council/. Accessed August 21, 2010.

Esaki, N., & Larkin, H. (2013). Prevalence of adverse childhood experiences (ACEs) among child service providers. *Families in Society, 94(1)*: 31.

Esaki, N., Benamati, J., Yanosy, S., Middleton, J., Hopson, L., Hummer, V., & Bloom, S. L. (2013). The Sanctuary Model: Theoretical framework. *Families in Society, 94(2)*: 29–35.

Felitti, V. J., & Anda, R. F. (2010). The relationship of adverse childhood experiences to adult medical disease, psychiatric disorders, and sexual behavior: Implications for healthcare. In: R. Lanius, E. Vermetten, & C. Pain (Eds.), *The Impact of Early Life Trauma on Health and Disease: The Hidden Epidemic* (pp. 77–87). New York: Cambridge University Press.

Finkelhor, D., Turner, H., Ormrod, R., Hamby, S., & Kracke, K. (2009). Children's exposure to violence: A comprehensive national survey. Juvenile Justice Bulletin, October. Available at: www.ncjrs.gov/pdffiles1/ojjdp/227744.pdf. Accessed January 3, 2010.

Gastil, J. (1993). Democracy in Small Groups: Participation, Decision Making, and Communication. Philadelphia, PA: New Society Publishers.

Glaze, L. E., & Maruschak, L. M. (2008). Parents in prison and their minor children. Bureau of Justice Statistics Special Report, NCJ 222984. Available at: www.ojp.usdoj.gov/bjs/pub/pdf/pptmc.pdf. Accessed January 30, 2009.

Groves, B., Zuckerman, B., Marans, S., & Cohen, D. J. (1993). Silent victims: Children who witness violence. *Journal of the American Medical Association, 269*: 262–264.

Hammond, S. A., & Mayfield, A. B. (2004). The Thin Book of Naming Elephants: How to Surface Undiscussables for Greater Organizational Success. Bend, OR: Thin Book Publishing Company.

Hoge, M. A., Morris, J. A., Daniels, A. S., Stuart, G. W., Huey, L. Y., & Adams, N. (2007). An Action Plan on Behavioral Health Workforce Development: A Framework for Discussion, The Annapolis Coalition on the Behavioral Health Workforce. Rockville, MD: Substance Abuse and Mental Health Services Administration, U.S. Department of Health and Human Services.

Jones, M. (1968). *Beyond the Therapeutic Community: Social Learning and Social Psychiatry*. New Haven, CT: Yale University Press.

Knudsen, E. I., Heckman, J. J., Cameron, J. L., & Shonkoff, J. P. (2006). Economic, neurobiological, and behavioral perspectives on building

America's future workforce. *Proceedings of the National Academy of Science, 103(27)*: 10155–10162.

Li, X., Howard, D., Stanton, B., Rachuba, L., & Cross, S. (1998). Distress symptoms among urban African-American children and adolescents: A psychometric evaluation of the checklist of children's distress symptoms. *Archives of Pediatrics and Adolescent Medicine, 152*: 569–577.

Marmot, M. (2004). *The Status Syndrome: How Social Standing Affects Our Health and Longevity*. New York: Holt.

McEwen, B. S., & Gianaros, P. J. (2010). Central role of the brain in stress and adaptation: Links to socioeconomic status, health, and disease. *Annals of the New York Academy of Sciences, 1186*: 190–222.

News, C. (2012). Census: U.S. poverty rate spikes, nearly 50 million Americans affected. Available at: http://washington.cbslocal.com/2012/11/15/census-u-s-poverty-rate-spikes-nearly-50-million-americans-affected/. Accessed November 15, 2012.

NIOSH. (2006). Workplace violence prevention, strategy and research needs. Cincinnati, OH: Department of Health and Human Services, Centers for Disease and Control Prevention, National Institute for Occupational Safety and Health. Available at: www.cdc.gov/niosh/conferences/work-violence. Accessed November 15, 2012.

Osofsky, J. D., Wewers, S., Hann, D. M., & Fick, A. C. (1993). Chronic community violence: What is happening to our children? *Psychiatry, 56*: 36–45.

Pascale, R. T., Millemann, M., & Gioja, L. (2000). *Surfing the Edge of Chaos: The Laws of Nature and the New Laws of Business*. New York: Crown Business.

Richters, J. E., & Martinez, P. (1993). The NIMH community violence project: I. Children as victims of and witnesses to violence. *Psychiatry, 56*: 7–21.

Rivard, J. C., Bloom, S. L., McCorkle, D., & Abramovitz, R. (2005). Preliminary results of a study examining the implementation and effects of a trauma recovery framework for youths in residential treatment. *Therapeutic Community. The International Journal for Therapeutic and Supportive Organizations, 26(1)*: 83–96.

Rivard, J. C., McCorkle, D., Duncan, M. E., Pasquale, L. E., Bloom, S. L., & Abramovitz, R. (2004). Implementing a trauma recovery framework for youths in residential treatment. *Child and Adolescent Social Work Journal, 21(5)*: 529–550.

Rivard, J. C., Bloom, S. L., Abramovitz, R. A., Pasquale, L., Duncan, M., McCorkle, D., & Fedel, S. (2003). Assessing the implementation and effects of a trauma-focused intervention for youths in residential treatment. *Psychiatric Quarterly, 74(2)*: 137–154.

Seibel, W. (1999). Successful failure: An alternative view of organizational coping. In: H. K. Anheier (Ed.), *When Things Go Wrong: Organizational Failures and Breakdowns* (pp. 91–104). Thousand Oaks: Sage.

Senge, P. (1994). *The Fifth Discipline: The Art and Practice of the Learning Organization*. New York: Doubleday.

Shonkoff, J. P. (2012). Leveraging the biology of adversity to address the roots of disparities in health and development. *Proceedings of the National Academy of Sciences, 109 (Supplement 2)*: 17302–17307.

Shonkoff, J. P., Garner, A. S., Siegel, B. S., Dobbins, M. I., Earls, M. F., McGuinn, L., Wood, D. L. (2012). The lifelong effects of early childhood adversity and toxic stress. *Pediatrics, 129(1)*: 2011–2663.

Shonkoff, J. P., Richter, L., van der Gaag, J., & Bhutta, Z. A. (2012). An integrated scientific framework for child survival and early childhood development. *Pediatrics, 129(2)*: 2011–0366.

Smith, K. K., Simmons, V. M., & Thames, T. B. (1989). "Fix the Women": An intervention into an organizational conflict based on parallel process thinking. *The Journal of Applied Behavioral Science, 25(1)*: 11–29.

CHAPTER SIX

"What happens after this quiet bit? I may have to leave now." The risks of empathy

Eleanor Richards

Wallace Stevens wrote a poem titled: "Peter Quince at the clavier" (1923). The poem moves on to be about something other than music in its direct sense, saying things about intrusion and welcome, fear and longing, which do have echoes for the piece of work at the centre of this chapter. But for now these opening lines stand alone:

> Just as my fingers on these keys
> Make music, so the self-same sounds
> On my spirit make a music, too.
> Music is feeling, then, not sound
> […]. (Stevens, 1923)

This chapter was originally prepared for a conference on the theme of empathy. That is a word I have never felt sure that I have understood or been wholly at ease with, perhaps because for me it implies a dimension in which the therapist may easily be afraid of failing or feeling inadequate. For that reason, perhaps, I found myself wanting to think about it in the context of a piece of continuing work with someone with whom the possibility of empathy has felt very remote at times (in both directions), and for whom the prospect of having his feelings recognised has been something he has striven to avoid.

So this is not particularly about technique, or even about how to think; it is about how we both might find sustenance and movement in what can often feel a rather bleak place. I think it is also an attempt to see how we might, both client and therapist, acknowledge and respond to the fears that arise within and between us and recognise what we can habitually do in the face of these.

I will call my patient Theo, as an abbreviation of Theodore. His own name has a comparable (to me) slightly archaic feel, and is often short-ened. What's more, Theodore means "gift of God" and there has been something very central in this work about Theo's sense of himself as the person who was meant to be a miraculous solution and grew up into a disappointment.

He is now twenty-two; we have known one another for two years. What has been painfully clear from the start is that he has profound difficulties in, and anxieties about, flexibly and openly relating to oth-ers, and little faith in himself; and that the depth of his trauma and loss in childhood has had some implications for his broader development. He was never very successful at school but, more widely, I think he has been too fearful to allow himself to learn from experience in any way that might allow him more faith in the restorative and developmen-tal possibilities of relationships. To learn anything at all is to change, and in that respect the only learning he is interested in is that which will increase and sustain his complicated and much needed defences. I have found it enormously important to remember that in the face of trauma the establishment of defences at all, whatever difficulties they may bring, is of itself a creative and developmental act and a gesture towards life.

Theo has been offered various other interventions in the past, aimed primarily at addressing some of his more risky behaviour. At various stages that has involved educational psychology, individual cognitive behavioural therapy, and group meetings for him, his parents, and teachers. He told me that he had found some of these things "rather interesting" and had sometimes made notes in sessions, I think perhaps in an attempt to organise and master something of his own disturbance, and to manage his anxiety in the sessions themselves. But his deep fears which have exacerbated his isolation from others have continued to dominate him.

Theo was adopted when he was eight months old by the people who from now on I will call his parents. His father is British, his mother American. They were living in New York at the time because his father was working there; both of them were also involved in an institute for the study of theology. They returned to the United Kingdom (UK) when Theo was ten. His father gave up his job, and was in due course ordained into a branch of the Christian church which has its roots in very ancient traditions, but has few members of British origin. Those British people who have joined it have generally done so because of its conservatism in terms of doctrinal matters and its views on issues of marriage and gender relations, which have offered a haven to those troubled by some of the more liberal developments in other churches. It also has a tradition of worship which places great emphasis on the proper conduct of liturgy and ceremonial, and takes place in richly dec- orated buildings. Similarly, it has an ancient musical tradition, but that is one which once again places great emphasis on the proper perform- ance of long-valued material, but is not open to adaptation or inno- vation. There seems to be a lot of theology, but much less about the personal dimension of religious experience. I dwell on this, no doubt rather selectively, because it strikes me as a useful metaphor for Theo's experience and self: someone who presents an external appearance of articulacy, organisation, and cultural plenty, but within whom there is little apparent place for curiosity, or questions, or the unexpected.

Theo is reported to have done well in the early months of his life with his birth mother, who was a single parent; he was separated from her abruptly when she received a prison sentence for theft. There are photos of him with her, some of which he has shown to me; he appears there as an alert, engaged baby, in ordinary inventive and playful dialogue with her. After the sudden separation he spent some weeks in a care facility run by the United States social services (more like an orphanage than foster care) before coming to the attention of an adoption agency and so to his parents. They were childless, in their early forties, and he was their chance.

The family "story" about him, which he knows very well, is that when he reached his adoptive family he cried continually, resisted sleep, and refused comfort. He will say, as if it's part of a funny story (and perhaps now with some angry pleasure): "They had a hard time with me". In time, he did become quieter; in fact he became more and more with- drawn ("My mother says I was unfriendly"), and not much interested in stimulus beyond himself; one of his favourite activities was to beat a steady, unchanging rhythm on a toy drum, but he stopped immediately if anyone wanted to join in with him. Any intervention in his self-derived regulatory apparatus was much too endangering. Some of his ordinary milestones appeared late, and his speech, as it emerged, took the form of rather sophisticated, "learnt" talk, which his parents welcomed. "My parents are proud that I knew so many long words". Even hearing this much left me with a great sense of emptiness, struggling to respond other than in platitudes. It seemed that he gave up on protest and sought other means, however partial and distorted, to form a connection. The strongest attachment he could make to his parents was to try to be like them, and by that means absolutely joined onto them (in adult life he dresses conservatively and, like his father, has a beard). But to be joined onto someone only through external things, without any investment in their meaning for themselves and for oneself, renders it impossible, perhaps, to find the place of mutual exchange and collaboration that characterises something more secure.

He was at school in New York and then the UK until he was sixteen. His memories of that time suggest a young man with no friends, who was routinely bullied and teased, and had occasional aggressive outbursts of his own. Thereafter he tried various jobs but nothing lasted: his increasingly rigid and idiosyncratic patterns of behaviour and his growing aggressiveness whenever he felt under pressure ensured that. When he felt that his performance at work was found wanting, he would respond with angry shouting and occasional threats of violence.

He lived with his parents until three years ago, and then, encouraged by them, moved into a shared house. The double bind of wanting to do what they wanted, whilst feeling the recurring terror of rejection implicit in the plan, was very hard for him to manage. He responded in part by losing all interest in his physical wellbeing, allowing his room and himself to become dirty, and establishing a daily routine for himself of drifting from coffee shop to coffee shop until he ran out of money. More recently he has lived in a flat on his own, where things have gone better. He has a part time job working for a company that repairs computers, and maintains a very fixed weekly routine, which includes attendance at our meetings.

My first sense of Theo was of someone who could not be still. As I went to the waiting room to meet him I was aware of sounds of movement and of things being dropped, which turned out to be him reorganising some of the things in his backpack. When we reached the room and began to talk I realised that this constant movement was central to him; he shifted in his chair, crossed and re-crossed his legs, gestured with his arms, and looked anxiously around. For myself, I could find no good way to settle my body either. If I made an effort to sit still it seemed unnaturally calm and distant, and if I spoke with any animation or made gestures of my own, it felt somehow overactive and distracting. I could not find a natural place to be.

As Theo began to speak, I was met by a torrent of rapid and anxious talk, which began with him announcing that he had been looking forward to meeting me. From then on, his talk was repetitive, not only in content but in specific pieces of phraseology, and it consisted largely of information. There were three topics: the first was his life story so far, which he assumed I would want to know. He recounted it rather flatly and routinely, not really seeking any response, and with no apparent sense of the impact it might have. The other two were life in his father's church and congregation, and classical music. These are also his parents' prevailing preoccupations. The church talk was about organisational matters and internal disputes, and the talk of music was about various composers and their output, together with a succession of critical opinions of various performers. If the talk had a prevailing flavour, it was of a clinging to authority (rather dismissive views of various orchestras) or of powerful inside knowledge (anticipation of the downfall of various church members). The world and other people were to be observed and commented on from a distance, but not met and experienced. I wondered how he had perceived his parents' ways of talking about him. It all felt desperate, and there was something painfully ironic in his need to speak about such a potentially enriching thing as music with such defensive critical detachment.

There is something in Theo's dealings with music that has echoes, in its own terms, for me. Classical music is in my background too, and in a big way. At an earlier stage in my life I earned my living, and, as I believed, a sense of my identity, from my involvement in music performance and in musicology. Both scholarship and the playing of music were represented by my parents' choices of lifelong professional activity. A big task for me has been to find my own relationship with music, and to separate my passion for it from its place in the attachment patterns in my own family, and my need to feel connected to them through those things (in other words, to find a musical voice that was mine). So something in Theo's own need to find his voice has been very immediate for me, and the frequent appearance of music in our talk has heightened that.

Theo always arrives with several plastic carrier bags and a backpack. These contain a large collection of CDs (of classical music) and a portable CD player with headphones. He needs to bring these into the room with him. The sense both of the literal weight of all this, and of its hard edged, armoured quality, in tactile terms, is very great, as is, of course, its function as a wall between him and new or unexpected experience. The sounds and the solitary regulation they offer him, in coffee shops or pubs (supposedly social places) also fill the emptiness. I suspect he is never without headphones unless he is talking himself.

His musical choices are narrowly defined; he likes baroque music, usually just for instruments. I think the human voice is too painful for him. The music he likes has some striking characteristics (familiar in the idioms of Handel or Vivaldi, for instance): it has a clear and steady pulse, often moving in blocks of four or eight bars, its sound world is consistent (no instruments dropping in and out), and so is its emotional world. There are no sudden changes of mood. Within that rather hastily described frame, of course, can appear music of tremendous emotional power, but I think it is the frame itself that sustains Theo.

At times, Theo affects the assurance and fluency of an adult young man. His vocabulary is sophisticated and his language idiomatic. He can speak with an air of assumed authority, especially when, as often, delivering information or opinions. He has a repertoire of gestures which include a rather world-weary shrug, and a way of shaping his hand when making a point; after saying something he may lean back in his chair and look at me with what sometimes feels like the scrutiny of a tutor waiting for an answer.

Donnel Stern (1994, p. 458) refers to those whom he describes as "uncommunicative and affectively disengaged patients, people who have great difficulty formulating their experience". For such people, the language that does emerge can be experienced as stilted and impoverished, and it can function more as a sharp reminder of the "enclosed" quality of the patient's feelings and, equally, of the "excluded" experience of the listening therapist. To continue to struggle for greater verbal freedom and understanding may simply leave us feeling ever more constrained and uncertain of our capacity to meet. Theo needs very much to sound coherent; what often emerges is a painful mixture of rather sophisticated forms of words and a sense that these phrases are not his own. They are a heard and borrowed idiom which heightens my own sense of the emptiness (or rather the unrepresentable experience) that lies behind them. They seem to be part of an effort to appear real and to generate a response in me, but often I can simply feel that I am being asked to play a continuing role in the pseudo-relational drama that he has felt required to be part of all his life, in which we are both in some measure acting. He is ill at ease without his usual script; if I do not come up with things that fit with that, he is lost.

Early on Theo sometimes told me that our work together might well not last. He is very used to being sent from one professional (or, as he might rather bitterly say, "one concerned person") to another, and told me that that is what I would do in the end. The implication was that I, too, would find him a disappointment and would rescue myself by doing things on my terms; that is, discharging him. At moments at which he could allow himself to hear something of warmth or just ordinary interest from me, he found it hard to bear, and needed to burst in with more statements and opinions. How can he separate the welcomeness of an empathic response from the irreversible intrusion of a demand? Perhaps his experience has been that at such moments he has been briefly awake to his intense longing for such connection and so, immediately, too in touch with his rage at the lack of it and the dangers of his rage towards those from whom he seeks it. In our encounters, therefore, we were faced with his desire for an experience of mutuality which was driven aside by his impulse to lonely destructiveness.

Theo has an ordinary longing to be known; because I appear to welcome him and attend to him, it must be, in his view, that I do not yet know him properly. My moment of disappointment is bound to come sooner or later. If I were to refer Theo elsewhere, it would confirm his conviction, born of defensive despair, that, as he would say, "It's no good", and it would bring him some satisfaction. It would add me to the list of people who have ended up fitting into his familiar pattern of events—and an unchanging pattern, however bleak, is more secure than the uncertainties of a more open future.

At the same time, Theo continues to come, and that of itself highlights his sharp inner conflict: on the one hand it is part of his assumption that he is playing his part in the familiar narrative of moving towards one more bad ending; on the other hand, he has begun to find, in spite of himself, that glimpses of something else are beginning to find a more secure place. To allow himself to be a little freer would bring the fear of losing all contact with others, who he believes can only know him as he is. To remain as he is risks not only the familiar old disappointment, but potentially the collapse, or at the very least the turning away of the other, confirming his dread of himself as the bearer of dangerously destructive possibilities which will not only destroy the very fragile external structure that he is so dependent upon, but will also, as he has more recently said, "break me inside".

To paraphrase something Theo has said, or, even more, to offer something approaching an interpretation, invites rejection. It is felt as an attack on his existing scheme of things because it does not reproduce it exactly, so it is as if I have turned away. Early on he talked about his father's anger when he gets something wrong in church (he is an acolyte and is involved in ceremonial): "He yelled at me afterwards and said I had delayed proceedings". I said (probably thinking much more widely about Theo's impact on his father's life): "Something happened and you disrupted the smooth running of things". Theo said: "No, I delayed proceedings".

So I must not be inventive, even in finding new words, and nor can he be.

If he were to stop being as he is he might be forgotten. His urgent need to maintain a relational "status quo" by seeking to repeat familiar scenarios has its roots in his deep doubt that he can really be "seen" in any other way. If he were to change, who would he be? Would anyone know him at all? If the pain underlying his behaviour were to be recognised more directly, would that somehow diminish it, or make it a thing of the past? Then what would be left? Perhaps nothing, in his imagination, or, worse, some dreaded and as yet unknown Theo that he can only imagine would be intolerable to us both. The dazed, separated baby perhaps learnt very early that protest and distress were uncontainable. Better to keep silent, or to turn to the unchanging "drumming"— literally—in the nursery, and later transmuted into rigid repetition and factual preoccupations. It has been salutary for me recognise the nature of my own fear of being ignored, and of the rise of feelings in me of being dull and useless. At such moments I can distance myself from the powerful emotional communication that that experience is bringing, and retreat into theorising, or casting around for technique.

Somehow Theo must find that this is not too much for us both to bear. For me to continue to sound, as he requires, rather like his parents, reassures him that I am keeping going. If they manage their psychic pain by turning to their familiar regulatory patterns and interests, then that is what regulates him too. For him, "thought" only means appearing calm and reflective, reiterating pieces of knowledge, or dealing in abstractions.

So ordinary dialogue is difficult. To pick up something of Theo's and make something of it, or add to it something of my own, is to take something away from him. He feels anything approaching playfulness or experiment as an abandonment; I must reflect back accurately what is said. If I don't, the tension in the room rises quickly: Theo clenches his fists, looks downwards, and tightens his breathing. The irony is that such a response in me may well come from a place of empathy; something in the tone of his communication to me has allowed me to feel more free in myself, and I have responded from myself with ordinary aliveness. As Donnel Stern says "Every act of hearing, knowing or understanding is an interpretation" (1994, p. 443). The composer John Cage, says much the same thing when he points out that "there is no meaning in what we (the musicians) do, other than what is determined by each one who hears it" (Meyer, 1956). Those moments in which I respond with something of my own are evidence of my aliveness, which is a source of such alarm to Theo.

For Theo, the prevailing climate has been that of the shared idioms of talk that is his parents'. To join in and be welcomed has required him to learn that language is the hope that at least his external self can be recognised. This is a fragile attachment, in the course of which he seems to have learnt that to surprise or confront others on the level of feeling risks damage to them and so to his sense of his value. The secure enough child's capacity to explore, in the assurance that his return, in some ways in a new form created by his embracing of new experience, will be welcomed with pleasure and curiosity, does not seem to have been a possibility for him. Instead he has had to cling to a framework that is not his own and which he cannot be sure will bear the strain put upon it by his life of feeling.

In the middle of last year, Theo was faced with the real possibility of loss. His father had a heart attack. He was admitted to hospital and Theo was told that he must not visit him because he might be disruptive and distressing. Suddenly he was faced with others' fantasy (and his own) that just by being himself he might kill someone. He was terribly hurt, and that emerged when we met in loud, rhythmic repetitions of: "I must be there. It will be OK. I don't get it; I must be there". These are powerful words in themselves, but what I also felt very aware of was their very different rhythmic shape. Theo normally talks in rather long, careful sentences: here was something much more broken up, loud, and abrupt—and emotionally immediate.

I surprised myself by feeling suddenly less bothered about "getting it right" or simply confirming what he had said and I found myself responding quite ordinarily: "You want to be with him and be his son." Theo's body moved away from its rigid, upright posture and shallow breathing; he sat back in his chair with a long out breath and slowly said "Be his son", and looked up at me steadily. We were able momentarily to hold between us his longing, not only for his father at that moment, but for something much more far reaching that was lost. In accepting my response without correcting me or distancing himself, but recognising its emergence from what had preceded it, he had allowed our exchange to generate something new. He had let himself be recognised, and in doing that had given me the freedom to recognise him, and to be a separate person who might have something to offer him. What he offered me in that moment was the chance to feel more alive. There was a pause and then he said something like the words which form the title of this chapter. "What happens after this quiet bit? I may have to leave now."

I think, looking back, that the "musical" dimension of that exchange was a central part of it. He had produced some short, abrupt phrases: I had responded with something quieter and slow moving. I experienced that moment not just as a glimpse of an emotional possibility which might be nourishing for us both, but as something which shifted the aesthetic quality of our exchanges. I don't know which brought about the other, but there was something in that moment, or in whatever had made it possible, which freed me to listen differently. Quite simply, I began to attend more actively, and with enjoyment, to the pace, tone, and pulse—the musicality—of our exchanges.

In the following session Theo returned to the news of his father and I told him that I thought the way we had talked about it the previous week had been important. He said "Yes … our voices felt different". (not "were different"). I said "… and we heard that they were different."

All this reminds me of some useful words from Anne Alvarez. She is writing about the shift from the old traditional model of psychoanalysis to something more immediate and relational, and puts it like this:

The popular image of the zipper-mouthed, detached, and frosty analyst-scientist really no longer applies. The comparison, instead, should perhaps be with a trained and skilled but constantly improvising musician who, like the patient, has to live and learn from felt experience and—not surprisingly—also from practice. (Alvarez, 1992, p. 3)

In a paper at the 2003 John Bowlby conference, "Touch, attachment, and the body" Colwyn Trevarthen talked about the musicality of mother/infant dialogue. He pointed out the rhythmic flow of sound and gesture and the real aesthetic pleasure for the pair in varying and developing their repertoire. Musicality is in all of us, and having a sense of rhythm is nothing to do with being good on the dance floor. Perhaps a sense of rhythm rests much more in the ability to walk down a crowded pavement without bumping into anyone; in other words, in the capacity to feel and anticipate the flow of events and the rhythmic styles and shifts of oneself and other people. Musicality is relational.

But what happens when that ready mutual improvising is disrupted or goes awry? Those familiar videos of mother/baby pairs show quickly that when the mother's attuned response is missing, or not quite in the right tone, or just half a second late, the baby is terribly thrown. He may flop and lose energy and curiosity, or he may tighten up and try to hold himself together in rigid bodily experience.

For a long time with Theo, I had felt that his dread of misattunement, to put it in those terms, was so great that he had made the rigid, armoured position his own to ensure that he was safe from such losses. My job, in his eyes, was simply to help him perpetuate that. Certainly our early conversations were full of pavement collisions: we cut across one another, misjudged pauses, stopped and started, and so on. But the more I let myself attend to the sound quality of our exchanges—our voices, pace, rhythm, emphases, and how those emerged in our speech and in our bodies—the more I felt our ordinary musicality. It became possible to listen with less anxiety and more sensory curiosity.

Music is notoriously—and unsurprisingly—difficult to talk about. We can describe it in technical terms, analyse its structures, put it in its historical context, compare it with other music, and so on. But what is actually going on? We can find some words but we may have, as Eliot (1944) says, "had the experience but missed the meaning". And in all that discussion or technical analysis of music are we not only serving our ordinary cultural interests, but also trying to find a means to manage the enormity of the absolute and undeniable life of feeling that music asserts? By its very nature, music, in the way it is understood and thought about in the West, is something that may give any of us, when we think about how we relate to it, some clues about ourselves. Music faces us with wordless sounds which seem to mean something to us.

Music, like therapy, (or any conversation) moves through time. Its patterns of rhythm and pitch and harmony generate anticipation of what may happen next. As the music moves along, those expectations may be satisfied, denied, or made to wait.

> Music can generate allusion to future possibilities of things unfolding; when those future possibilities become actualities, the significance of those earlier events may become clear, their sense (at least partially) disambiguated, giving rise to what Mayer (1956) has called music's "evident meanings". (Cross & Morley, in: Malloch & Trevarthen, 2009, p. 69)

Music's "floating intentionality" (ibid. p. 70) within oneself or with others, may allow it to embrace within a single statement disparate areas of feeling or experience in a way that does not allow them to be separated out into separate propositions. On one level, this may be the playing together of two instruments that do not sound alike; the contribution of neither makes sense on its own and the sound-world they create between them can exist only in their connectedness (this may be what Theo and I did in the exchange about his father. We brought different idioms and they came together to make a moment of meaning). In a broader sense, a movement of a big classical symphony (by Beethoven or Brahms, for instance), has as its central purpose the voicing of a succession of mood states, an investigation of what may happen when they engage with one another, and what the transformative possibilities of that drama may be.

If this all sounds familiar and reminiscent of the dynamic flow and energy of feeling in the consulting room, perhaps that is not surprising. But music, like the therapy session, needs its boundaries, and the emotional power of music rests not only in its sounds but in its shape.

Our expectations of what may happen next rest in part in our familiarity with the idiom of the music, and when an expected resolution is not reached or the music changes direction, it is because of the arrival of a dissonance (a note that disrupts the harmony). Dissonance is disturbing, but it is what makes change possible; without it, the music stays stuck in a repetitive bland cycle that lacks the aggressive drive for life. It is striking, incidentally, that it was at the end of the nineteenth century that some composers began more radically to investigate dissonance for its own sake, with less concern for maintaining the familiar harmonic world they had inherited. At that same time, as Stein points out, Freud was proposing the project of psychoanalytic listening:—"to listen to the sounds of human experience in a radically different and profoundly deeper way" (1999, p. 1).

Christopher Bollas (1987, p. 28) suggests that the infant's early experience of reverie is not only secure and containing: it is the beginning of the discovery of aesthetic pleasure. This brings not just enjoyment, but creative excitement, because the experience of being with the mother or primary caregiver is felt as a source of growth and transformation. I think that when Theo and I first met, and he said he had been looking forward to our meeting, he was perhaps not simply being civil, but voicing some much more unformulated hope that this relationship might be one in which he could feel transformation and life.

So, little by little, it is the shape and feel of conversation with Theo that has begun to change. He has begun to allow himself simply to hear my voice, and to let himself return to that state in which my words matter much less for what they say, and more for their simple confirmation of the presence of someone else with whom he can—occasionally—improvise.

There are still plenty of times when he needs to move into the familiar anxious factual delivery, but there are also times at which we can experiment with the ordinary pleasure of stops and starts, or hesitations, or moments of suspense about who is going to speak next. If one of us cuts across the other, or we both start to speak at the same moment, the mistiming can feel enjoyable rather than disastrous. Theo can catch my eye and raise an eyebrow in recognition.

My inner "sound" experience has changed, too. In the early days of knowing Theo, I often found that I was inventing musical phrases in my mind as we talked and "playing" them over and over again. They had rather neat conclusions, but somehow they didn't develop—some kind of regulation for me, but also reflective of the shape of our talk. More recently, they have fallen silent, and I have had better ears for what takes place between us. Theo's gestures and bodily unsettledness continue, but there are times, too, when he can be more still and physically balanced, or when his gestures and movement are a more integrated, connected part of what is happening.

The broader rhythm of the work is also something we can recognise. Theo will recall events from earlier sessions, sometimes rather impressionistically ("That sounds like that time when we were talking about …") so that we can start to feel links and allow ourselves to know more actively the creative connection between events. I think that apprehension of the broader pace of things (and this is slow work) is vital. Without it, we risk falling into another kind of fixed pattern, in which steady familiar talk may occasionally be punctuated by something more exciting and immediate, but fundamentally we do not expect much beyond that to change. That is a dead end. But if we can begin to have some trust in the move through and beyond knowledge (Theo's and mine) towards whatever is our version of something approaching wisdom, then there are possibilities.

Here is the philosopher Susanne Langer talking about music:

> Music is revealing, where words are obscuring, because it can have not only a content but a transient play of contents. It can articulate feelings without becoming wedded to them [...] The assignment of meanings is a shifting, kaleidoscopic play, probably below the threshold of consciousness, certainly outside the pale of discursive thinking. The lasting effect is [...] *to make things conceivable* rather than to store up propositions. Not communication but insight is the gift of music; in a very naïve phrase, a knowledge of "how feelings go". (Langer, 1942, pp. 243–244)

"How feelings go". For Theo, to name feelings is to neutralise them, in terms of his felt relationship to them in talk. The words become recruited into his large and intricate vocabulary, but their connection with his inner experience is severed, if it was ever there, and they are turned to some anti-creative purpose. But perhaps our attention to the way we are in the moment ("how feelings go") can bring structure and order to the contents of his experience in a way that can let it be more felt and thought about, and less pushed away or frozen (Alvarez, 1992, p. 4).

"Patient and therapist evolve a type of poetry that is special to that patient and that therapist in their particular and unique relationship" (Meltzer, 1992, in: Williams, 1997, p. 43). It is the nature of this poetic flow itself which demonstrates the meaning of experience. But it's a meaning not discovered through the usual kind of negotiation which might bring a shared understanding of words. That sort of negotiation could fall into endless circling in a rather closed place—something Theo knows well and both loves and hates—but that closed place is not where real communication takes place, internally, or between two people. The truth discovered by inspiration (literally the breathing in of something new) is not a final, agreed quality—again, something Theo wants and dreads—but it is the meaning of a particular intersubjective situation at a particular time, and that is what we need to know for movement to become possible.

For me and Theo, empathy—if that is what it is—can be in shared moments of creative experience, felt mostly outside the words. The recognition inherent in those is what gives us some freedom.

The French composer Pierre Boulez, who has written thousands of analytic (in another sense) words about music and its performance, recently and reassuringly said this: "As experience grows and life goes by, you can do less thinking and are more able simply to exist within the music" (Boulez, in: Vermeil, 2003).

References

Alvarez, A. (1992). *Live Company*. London: Brunner-Routledge.

Bollas, C. (1987). *The Shadow of the Object*. London: Free Association.

Cross, I., & Morley, I. (2009). The evolution of music: Theories, definitions and the nature of the evidence. In: S. Malloch, & C. Trevarthen (Eds.), *Communicative Musicality* (pp. 61–81). Oxford: OUP.

Eliot, T. S. (1944). The Dry Salvages. In: *Four Quartets*. London: Faber and Faber.

Langer, S. (1942). *Philosophy in a New Key*. Cambridge: Harvard.

Malloch, S., & Trevarthen, C. (2009). *Communicative Musicality*. Oxford: Oxford University Press.

Meltzer, D. (1992). *The Claustrum*. Perthshire: Clunie Press.

Meyer, L. (1956). *Emotion and Meaning in Music*. London: University of Chicago Press. Available at: http://painterskeys.com. Accessed: August 15, 2013.

Stein, A. (1999). Well-tempered bagatelles: A meditation on listening in psychoanalysis and music. *American Imago, 56(4)*: 387–416.

Stern, D. (1994). Empathy is interpretation (and whoever said it wasn't?). *Psychoanalytic Dialogues, 4(3)*: 441–471.

Stevens, W. (1923). Peter Quince at the clavier. In: *Collected Poems of Wallace Stevens* (1982). New York: Vintage Books.

Vermeil, J. (2003). *Thoughts on Conducting: Interviews with Pierre Boulez.* London: Amadeus Press.

Williams, M. (1997). Inspiration: A psychoanalytic and aesthetic concept. *British Journal of Psychotherapy, 14(1)*: 33–43.

CHAPTER SEVEN

Empathy and earned security: reciprocal influences, ruptures, and shifts in the psychotherapeutic process

Anastasia Patrikiou

Hermann Lotze, German philosopher and logician (1817–1881), in his excerpt below, illustrates evocatively the process by which we perceive our environment, both animate and inanimate. He describes how we pour ourselves into the object in order to be and feel like the object we are contemplating. How we become the mollusc "in the monotonous pleasure of its openings and closings", in order to comprehend, perceive, understand and interpret it, and how during this process, the object inhabits us.

> No form is so resistant that our fancy cannot, living with it [...] place itself into It [...]. Thus we are able, furthered by the help of our sensations, to understand the alien, silent form, too. And we not only penetrate into the peculiar vital feelings of those which by kind and nature are near to us, into the joyful flight of the singing bird or the charming motion of the gazelle; we not only contract the feelers of our mind to the smallest thing, to dream with [...] the narrowly defined existence of the mollusc and the monotonous pleasure of its openings and closings; we not only extend ourselves, expanding with [...] them, into the slender forms

of the tree whose thin branches the pleasure of graceful bending and swaying animates; rather, even on to lifeless things we transfer these interpretive feelings and transform through them the dead weights and supports of buildings into so many limbs of a living body, whose inner tensions come back to us. (Lotze, 1858, pp. 200–201)

Lotze's view of how we understand the world is echoed in Carl Rogers' description of the empathic process with another:

> An empathic way of being with another person has several facets. It means entering the private perceptual world of the other and becoming thoroughly at home in it. It involves being sensitive, moment by moment, to the changing felt meanings which flow in this other person, to the fear or rage or tenderness or confusion or whatever he or she is experiencing. It means temporarily living in the other's life, moving about in it, delicately without making judgements; it means sensing meanings of which he or she is scarcely aware. (Rogers, 1980, p. 142)

In this paper I would like to look at how the presence or absence of empathy in the therapist impacts the therapeutic dyad. I will argue that, even though I do not agree with the Rogerian premise that empathy is the ultimate aim in therapy; I believe that it is Carl Rogers' definition and analysis of empathy which best describes the process as a felt, embodied state. The complexity present in the empathic process is often overlooked. "Being empathic" is frequently thought of as a state the therapist "naturally" inhabits. Empathy is considered to be a backdrop, a context in which therapy happens. Such an unreflected and unexplored view of empathy, I believe, impoverishes communication in the therapeutic relationship and misses opportunities for expanded understanding and growth. As Ferenczi (1928), Rogers (1951), and Kohut (1959) showed, this embodied state of empathy is not arrived at easily and demands a lot from the therapist.

I am proposing that empathy, as advocated by Rogers, has a significant role to play within a relational psychoanalytic context, in the form of *empathic moments*. During these moments the therapist's self is momentarily *suspended* in order to create a space for that deep listening process which I believe is at the forefront of therapeutic change.

I will try to illustrate this in a clinical example, after providing a brief historical overview of the concept of empathy.

The roots of empathy

The concept of empathy has become very much a part of everyday language now. However its current ordinariness belies the complexity, both in defining it and in elucidating the experiential and dynamic interplay between subject and subject or between subject and object. Definitions of empathy appear in many discourses, both scientific and non-scientific. Psychoanalytic literature contains a number of attempts to define this elusive concept (Sharma, 1992).

The word "empathy" has its linguistic roots in Greek and its conceptual roots in German aesthetic philosophy from the end of the nineteenth century, (Stueber, 2013). Romantic thinkers such as Johann Herder and Novalis had, in the eighteenth century, described ways of understanding the objects of art and nature through the processes of "feeling into" and poetic identification, in order to grasp their underlying spiritual essence. This was a reaction to Enlightenment thinkers, who stressed that investigation and understanding come about through the dissection and analysis of the physical characteristics of the object.

In 1873 Robert Fischer (1847–1933) a German philosopher, introduced the word *Einfühlung* (in-feeling, or, feeling into), to describe these processes of perception, and thought it a worthy enough concept for philosophical investigation. Philosopher, Theodore Lipps (1851–1914) made the leap from understanding *Einfühlung* as a concept fundamental to the aesthetic encounter, to one which he thought formed the primary mechanism for recognising others as creatures with a mind (Stueber, 2013). German philosophers explained that our aesthetic appreciation of objects were based on psychological processes evoked through our senses. Lipps understood *Einfühlung* as a phenomenon of "inner imitation" in which the mind mirrors the mental activities or experiences of another person as we observe their bodily activities or facial expressions. In his thinking he anticipated recent neuroscientific findings around mirror neurons as mechanisms of basic empathy (Stueber, 2013).

It was Edward Titchener (1867–1927), a British psychologist, who translated Lipps' idea of *Einfühlung* as "empathy" into the English language in 1909.

Empathy in the psychotherapeutic world

Freud

Freud was very much aware of the German aesthetic movement and was an admirer of Theodor Lipps. It is in *Jokes and their Relation to the Unconscious* (Freud, 1905c) that Freud first makes use of the concept of *Einfühlung* in trying to understand how empathy and comparison might be important parts "of the psychical processes of the comic" (Freud, 1905c, p. 187). Freud recognises *Einfühlung* as a process which allows us to understand others by putting ourselves in their place: the "analyst must adjust himself to the patient as a telephone receiver is adjusted to the transmitting microphone" (Freud, 1912e, pp. 115–116). He also sees *Einfühlung* as essential to establishing a good rapport with the patient and therefore a prerequisite for analysis. The patient's attachment to the analyst and the analysis will make him more receptive to the analyst's interpretations. Freud had a very intellectual view of empathy as he was generally averse to affective involvement by the therapist. His approach remained within a one-person psychology framework and was committed to a method based on rational, scientific investigation (Pigman, 1995).

Ferenczi

While a number of other analysts, such as Winnicott, Stack, Sullivan, Guntrip, Fairbairn, and others, developed theories based on the impact of the earliest relationship on the formation of the self, and within this context described many important elements of the empathic process, it was Sandor Ferenczi, Carl Rogers, and Heinz Kohut who developed theories of self and clinical practice based unambiguously on the concept of empathy (Rachman, 1988). Rachman says "In order to gain the necessary perspective on the capacities involved, one should consult the three major figures in the history of psychotherapy regarding empathic functioning—Sandor Ferenczi, Heinz Kohut, and Carl Rogers" (Rachman, 1988, p. 2).

Ferenczi, protégé, close colleague, and friend of Freud's, was particularly interested in developing analytic technique in the consulting room. Emotionally present, intuitive, warm, and innovative, Ferenczi focused on empathy as an important issue in psychoanalysis. The thoughts he developed around what it meant to be an empathic analyst were ground-breaking for his time (1924–1933). He demonstrated that in order to be such an empathic analyst, required special emotional and intellectual capacities. He says: "One gradually becomes aware of how immensely complicated the mental work demanded from the analyst is […]. One might say that his mind swings continuously between empathy, self observation, and making judgements" (Ferenczi, 1928, p. 96).

Ferenczi advocated the absence of all pretence. His distinctive empathic attunement enabled him to work with all patients. There were no "unsuitable" patients, which resulted in fellow analysts sending Ferenczi cases they could not work with. In "The elasticity of psychoanalytic technique" (Ferenczi, 1928), Ferenczi advocates changing the atmosphere in the session to one of warmth, kindness, and acceptance and was the first analyst to employ non-verbal cues to interpret unconscious process. He challenged the idea of the analyst as authority and began to see the therapeutic process as a collaboration in which the therapist is a participant. In this he was anticipating by many decades the thinking of American relational psychoanalysts. (Rachman, 1988).

Kohut

Heinz Kohut believed that psychopathology in patients was the result of parental empathic failure. This led to narcissistic injuries which impaired the individual from having an integrated sense of self. Responsiveness in the other was crucial for the functioning of the self and its cohesiveness. Kohut termed responsive others, "selfobjects" (Kohut, 1984). Phil Mollon poignantly describes this relationship with the selfobject as "the weaving of the self from the fabric of others" (Mollon, 2003, p. 17). Kohut believed that "the essence of the psychoanalytic cure resides in a patient's newly acquired ability to identify and seek out appropriate selfobjects—both mirroring and idealisable—as they present themselves in his realistic surroundings and to be sustained by them" (Kohut, 1984, p. 77). For Kohut, the therapist is to provide the patient with a selfobject experience which would correct earlier deficits. Kohut observed that his patients responded to empathic attunement in the therapist with an increased sense of wellbeing and mental functioning, and the opposite when there were lapses in empathy.

Kohut saw empathy not only as a way of fostering a warm nurturing environment, but as a way of gaining access to a patient's mental life. He called it "vicarious introspection" (Kohut, 1959). Breaking away from psychoanalytic tradition, Kohut became aware of the legitimacy of the patient's sense of reality as different to that of the therapist; he saw the therapist's task as being to see reality from the patient's perspective, by "feeling oneself into the life of another" (Kohut, 1984, p. 81). Kohut, an important figure in the psychoanalytic establishment and sometimes known as "Mr Psychoanalysis", struggled to disseminate his concepts because they were considered heretic" within the psychoanalytic world. In 1957 at a meeting at the Chicago Institute of Psychoanalysis he presented a paper in which he stated that empathy had a primary role in psychoanalysis. He was jeered and shouted down. It was only in 1971, in *The Analysis of the Self*, that he was able to publish a full account of his own take on personality theory and psychopathology and fell out of favour. In 1977 he abandoned Freudian drive theory altogether (Ellis & Abrahams, 2009).

Carl Rogers

Carl Rogers' unique contributions to the concept of empathy, which predated Kohut's, have largely been dismissed in the psychoanalytic community as "shallow and superficial" (Kahn & Rachman, 2000, p. 296). In the late 1930s Rogers was placing the client's sense of his own reality at the centre of the therapeutic endeavour and had become averse to interpretations of it. This was contrary to the psychoanalytic premise at the time which held that the client's problematic sense of reality was to be corrected through transference in the therapeutic relationship with the analyst, who was thought to have an objective view of the client's reality. Rachman states that Rogers' ideas were "simple, yet profound" (Kahn & Rachman, 2000, p. 295). Interestingly, Kohut and Rogers were both at Chicago University from 1945–1957, the former in the neurological and psychiatric department, the latter a professor in the psychology department. There was considerable ill feeling between the departments. Rogers described the animosity emanating from the psychiatric department without reference to Kohut. Kohut believed that counsellors in the psychology department merely applied superficial, reflective techniques in their work with patients. He did not acknowledge Rogers' contributions which in many cases bear a striking resemblance to his own, but neither does he acknowledge Ferenczi as having influenced him (Kahn & Rachman, 2000).

It is true that Rogers' analysis can seem simplistic alongside the complexity and sophistication of psychoanalytic thinking. However Rogers did what no other practitioner of psychotherapy had done: to hold a magnifying glass to the minutiae of the *experience* of human interaction and to examine what aspects in this interaction seemed meaningful, expanding, and therapeutic for the client. Rogers, like Ferenczi, believed that the kind of presence required of the therapist to develop, is not simple at all to attain, as it demands that she relinquishes all narcissistic wishes and designs for the client, as well as any pre-conceptions and judgements.

Away from psychoanalytic constraints, Rogers was able to delineate a theory of self and clinical practice, based on experiential processes and empirical data (Rogers, 1951). In 1942, he became the first to use audio-recordings in sessions. This enabled him and his counsellors to conduct a thorough post-session investigation of the material, specifically, the fine nuances within client-therapist interaction. Written records after a session by the therapist would always be distorted by a selective, subjective memory and would strip the account of the client's voice. Furthermore, counsellors were able to observe how their own responses and interventions aided or impeded the client's process. This practice prompts one to think of the work of Beatrice Beebe, (and others) who uses video recordings and feedback in her treatment of troubled parent–infant couples, in order to identify and work on the points at which communication fails or goes awry.

From his research and clinical work Rogers came to the conclusion that it was the therapist's empathic stance which created an environment in which the client was enabled to reach disavowed material, and in this way facilitated what he calls "personality change". He says:

> It is the individual [who] has within himself or herself vast resources for self understanding, for altering his or her self-concept, attitudes, and self-directed behaviour—and that these resources can be tapped if only a definable climate of facilitative psychological attitudes can be provided. (Rogers, 1986, p. 135)

He saw that an empathic stance, when genuinely authentic, was an incredibly delicate and complex process to manifest at relational depth. Rogers advocated that learning to be empathic, which he considered to be a way of being rather than a reflective technique (Rogers, 1980), was acquired through long experiential training in the following three conditions:

- Empathic listening and communication: the therapist is to accurately sense the thoughts, feelings, and personal meanings of the client's experience and communicates his understanding of these to the client in an accepting way. Rogers believed that in his most empathic state the therapist will be so immersed in the world of the client that he is able to clearly identify meanings that the client is aware of, but also meanings that are below his awareness (Rogers, 1986).
- Congruence: Rogers believed that growth in the client is facilitated if the therapist is genuinely herself in the relationship, and not veiled by the façade of a professional stance. Congruence/genuineness also means that the therapist is embodying the feelings and attitudes flowing in the intersubjective space. There is congruence between the felt experience of the client in the therapist, the therapist's awareness, and what he expresses to the client (Rogers, 1957).
- Unconditional positive regard: Rogers described this as a "non-possessive prizing" (Rogers, 1957) of the client. It means that the therapist communicates to the client that there are no conditions to his acceptance of him—"conditions of worth" (Rogers, 1986) imposed on us by others lead to pathology. The primary aim in therapy is to counteract the continuous struggle to fulfil the expectations of others, and this has a therapeutic effect. (Mearns & Thorne, 1988).

Rogers admits that the phrase "unconditional positive regard" may be an unfortunate phrase (Rogers, 1957) as it seems achievable only in theory. He says that in reality the effective therapist experiences *moments* of unconditional positive regard. At other times the therapist may experience conditional positive regard or even negative regard, which would require examination on the part of the therapist to ascertain whether this is due to interference of his own material or whether this reflects communications from the client. This experience may be addressed with the client, if appropriate, in a way which is helpful and congruent with the therapeutic relationship.

Relational psychoanalysts

Relational psychoanalysts such as Robert Stolorow, Bernard Brandcraft, and George Atwood firmly placed the therapeutic relationship within a two-person psychology framework. They looked at the work of Ferenczi, Rogers, and Kohut as they considered how the stance of the therapist could be altered from detached observer to participant, affecting, and affected. They emphasised Rogers' and Kohut's view of empathy as being an essential element of the therapeutic relationship and the client's sense of reality as valid and important. They differed from Rogers and Kohut with regards to their focus on the therapist's sense of his own reality and subjectivity and on the impact these had on the client and the relationship. In fact relational psychoanalysts proposed that the therapist, where appropriate, makes use of his experience relationally in a way that went beyond the transference and countertransference dynamic. For the relational psychoanalysts the relationship and how the two parties interact, is primary.

Relational psychoanalysts modelled their understanding of the therapeutic relationship on the caregiver-infant relationship. They drew on the work of thinkers such as Daniel Stern and Beatrice Beebe, who described how the subjectivities of the mother–infant dyad are instrumental in co-creating the relationship on which the infant depends for optimal development and growth. Like Rogerian therapists, relational psychoanalysts ask of the therapist to constantly monitor the vicissitudes of the relational dynamic inter-psychically and intra-psychically. Empathy in Rogerian terms is crucial in this interplay.

However for the relational psychoanalysts, an empathic state would not be enough to foster growth. Stolorow proposed an "active 'empathic inquiry" into the subjective life of the client, in order to bring about a reflective awareness in him with regards to how he "organises his experience" (Stolorow & Atwood, 1992, p. 370). Through empathic inquiry the therapist helps to shed light on a pre-reflective unconscious through suggestions and interpretations in order to help re-structure it. Unlike Rogers, Stolorow advocated a stance which aimed to help the client re-examine his existing "organisational structures" (Stolorow & Atwood, 1992)—what could be called "internal working models" in attachment terms. This was to be achieved through empathic attunement in the way that Rogers proposed, as well as through an engagement in appropriate and attuned suggestions and timely interpretations. Kahn suggests that Rogers stays with the deep listening process of the empathic moment, wanting to be a companion to the client as she makes the choices she wishes. Instead relational psychoanalysts actively propose, hopefully facilitating insights, which are the results of the client's conscious and unconscious, verbal and non-verbal, and bodily communications (Kahn, 1996).

The active involvement of the therapist's subjectivity in the therapeutic process implies that relational psychoanalysts think of impasses not only as events which convey some communication by the client, but as enactments co-created by both, affecting both, which are to be understood collaboratively and processed experientially within the relationship.

Empathy today

Work across an array of disciplines such as neurobiology, biochemistry, behavioural neurology, developmental psychology, developmental psychoanalysis etc., over the past two decades has brought to light the physiological basis of the empathic process and its essential role in human functioning (Schore, 1994). Scientific research has investigated the effects of the absence of empathy on the mental and psychological well-being of individuals and even on society in general (Baron-Cohen, 2011). This is perhaps a vindication of Ferenczi's, Rogers', and Kohut's preoccupation with empathy as a crucial ingredient in therapeutic communication and treatment.

Empathic moments and the suspension of self

When I was thinking about this paper, I was immediately reminded of my first felt experience of empathy at the start of my training as a therapist. It took place in a mock therapy session with a fellow trainee, who was my "client". When she started telling her story, I found myself feeling as if I was riding a wave with her, merged, rising and falling, bobbing and floating, as she guided me through her world of experiences, thoughts, and feelings. When the session came to an end I realised I had been in a sort of reverie and had lost touch with my surroundings momentarily. It was this embodied experience of empathy (*Einfühlung*) which allowed me to understand the nature and depth of the therapeutic connection and the power it had.

In her feedback my "client" said that she had felt "merged" with me, and how therapeutic the feeling was. How validating it was for her to feel that someone thought her "important enough", to take the trouble to merge with her sufficiently, to see and feel what she saw and felt.

My "client's" feedback corresponded with what Rogers said of the impact of such empathic moments: "Empathy dissolves alienation. For the moment, at least, the recipient finds himself or herself a connected part of the human race" (Rogers, 1980, p. 151).

What was happening for me?

I felt for the first time that I had been invited, as Mearns put it, "as a guest in the client's world" (Mearns, 2003, p. xi). Mearns in fact advises that a person–centred counsellor must always remember that she is a guest in the client's world. It felt like it was an honour to be there. I had already developed a number of preconceptions about my fellow student and wondered how possible it was for me to let go of my various formulations. However, I surprised myself. During those twenty minutes I really did suspend my preconceptions, prejudice, and judgement to make way for her. This was "unconditional positive regard" and it *could* be achieved in an empathic moment. In fact it seems impossible to *accurately* perceive the inner world of another without it. The journey she took me on made complete sense. All the problems and difficulties she described had perfect reasons to be there. Nevertheless, as Rogers himself said, it is doubtful whether this state of acceptance can be held for long, or even, and I add, whether it is optimal to do so.

The "merged" sense I described above, is an experiencing at relational depth, rather than talking (Mearns, 2003). A state of *Einfühlung*. This level of fine attunement, understanding, and acceptance gives the other a sense of personhood; a needed confirmation that one does exist as a separate, valued person with an identity.

Empathic impasse

Clinical illustration

Sara was a young woman in her late twenties who came to therapy because of how confused she felt about her relationship with her partner Kevin. Sara moved to the United States of America (USA) with her family from Lebanon, a country which has suffered from inter-communal strife. After completing her studies in the USA she joined a laboratory at a university here in the United Kingdom for post-doctoral studies. Sara and Kevin, a British man, had been living together for some time.

Like Kevin, Sara felt that marriage would be the next logical step in their relationship. However she had become embroiled in an internal conflict revolving around issues such as ethnicity, culture, religion, and difference. She was unable to make a commitment, but was also unable to leave the relationship. Kevin was agnostic and felt he had no problem converting to Sara's religion. Nevertheless Sara questioned his ability to share her "values" having not been born into her culture. Would these "innate" differences become a problem in the raising of children in the future?

Sara came from a family which was traumatically preoccupied with issues around religious and ethnic difference. She and her younger brother attended camps throughout childhood, which had a nationalistic and religious thrust.

Kevin was caring, warm, thoughtful, and attentive. However he questioned and challenged assumptions. This was in direct contrast to the background Sara had come from, which was structured around certainties and polarities. Being both in awe and resentful of this quality in Kevin, Sara experienced a powerful split between the part of herself that was embedded in the fabric of her cultural conditioning, and the other part which fantasised a world, where rigid codes of conduct were absent.

Sara's parents appeared to be generally accepting of a potential marriage to Kevin because he was willing to adopt the faith. I wondered if, like Sara, they unconsciously and consciously undermined the relationship, posing questions about his suitability and ability, to maintain and promote their specific cultural values.

Sara idealised family and community. She felt close to her mother but she was distant to her father who was a mariner and was away for months at a time. She felt him to be a stranger and intimidating when he was around. Her mother became the vitally important figure around which she shaped her life and whom she would not trouble more than necessary. Much of the family's emotional narrative was structured around this profound paternal absence. The mother was holding the family together and Sara was keenly aware of how her mother was having a "raw deal". The family was aided by an extended family network, particularly her father's younger brother and his wife and children. Essentially Sara had been emotionally neglected. There was no space for her needs, or sad and angry feelings.

Sara was bright and successful professionally, friendly, and sociable, but found it difficult to assert her inner desires. This was evident, even in our first session when I said to her "You want to comply, but you also want to do something meaningful for yourself". She immediately became tearful; throughout our work together, my reference to this internal conflict never failed to move her deeply. Below a bright exterior, she was deeply melancholic about her sense of her core self, as buried and entombed, unreflected, unmet, unrecognised, and uncelebrated.

We spent a substantial amount of time examining the close relationships in her life which, for a long time, were presented in their sugar-coated versions. She had been conditioned, after all, not to examine the negative, the sad, or the angry; except where it concerned Kevin. He became the denigrated, de-idealised object, which allowed her to keep family relationships intact. Whilst we reached her underlying resentments at the end of a session, it often felt like we started over again at the next. The process often reminded me of sand on a shore, on which we had made markings, only for the next wave to come and wipe it clean and restore it to its original pristine, unmarked state, as if nothing had happened.

In time, some of the positive gloss had faded and she was able to have a less schizoid view both of her family members and of Kevin. She also questioned her family's and community's narratives about religious and ethnic "enemies", and began exploring more complex ideas about real and imaginary friends and foes.

Although we had worked together for some time the therapeutic alliance was essentially tenuous. Again, below the gloss of the seeming connectedness, her polite, kind presence, and a desire to be supported and held, I had a strong sense that any form of attachment outside the family circle was considered a sort of a betrayal. I, in her mind, with her fantasies about my ethnic and religious differences, like Kevin, could never be really deeply connected to her. Transferentially this indicated her inability to connect with her own family; connections there, were held together by the glue of loyalty and obligation rather than by deep meaningful contact and tenderness.

In my countertransference response, I felt that on the one hand I was holding much of the outrage about the way in which her family attachments consistently proved to be so unsatisfying. On the other, I was beginning to bristle at Sara's treatment of Kevin and some of her beliefs which contained innate elements of bigotry and prejudice. In one particular session she spoke of Kevin's influence as "contaminating" and it was difficult not to think that she was speaking about my contaminating influence too. I found myself feeling deeply offended.

I was surprised at the intensity of my reaction to Sara's comments and at how threatening and de-stabilising her struggle was to me, how fragile and alive my feelings about prejudice still were as a white South African, and how easily my sense of earned security in this area was affected. I became aware of my own prejudices against Sara's background which I had kept at bay and had not properly acknowledged. I found that, unconsciously, I was structuring our therapeutic interchange around polar opposites too; religious dogma: bad—secularism: good, family impact: bad—therapy influence: good, closed societies: bad—open societies: good—and so on.

One particular session became a turning point in our work. Conflict was palpable in the room. Sara said that she was being punished through tormenting indecision and split loyalties, because she had veered from the traditional path of her community. At some point she asked aggressively whether I had any beliefs in anything at all. I was taken aback, unprepared, and asked her why it mattered to her. "Because I don't trust that you have my best interests at heart". In retrospect what I think she was saying was, "I am not sure that you are helping me achieve what will be ultimately good for me, but rather what *you* think is good for me, according to your belief system—about which I know nothing!" I was guilty of partisanship by being on the side of Sara that wanted to be free to grow and develop. I said clumsily that it would not be possible for me to share my beliefs with her but that I could understand how important it felt for her to know. The session ended with the intersubjective space seeming like a battlefield.

I had inadvertently been drawn into becoming a campaigner for what I believed was the correct outcome of the work. It is true that the strangled part of her was yearning for emancipation. But, were we to examine this from a Rogerian perspective, was that really her ultimate aim? Would it be her aim now? We had witnessed in the past year many growth moments, but what about the "not-for-growth moments"? (Mearns, 2003, p. 19). What about the protection of regressive steps?

Embedded in the client's splits and my own, I had ceased having an understanding of her inner world, and was therefore unable to have unconditional positive regard for her. I had stopped listening to all the parts, being partial to the ones I wanted to listen to. I was congruent with my own feelings but no longer mindful of what was relevant to the intersubjective space and her. In other words, I had stopped being empathic.

I was reminded of Mearn's idea that the embodied state of empathy entailed a deep, still listening; with no reflection, no interpretation, no inquiry (Mearns, 2003). It is in stillness that we can begin to hear again and it was to this stillness that I had to return.

In consultation with a colleague I was helped to connect with the embattled state triggered in me by the transference of the rigidities and splits in my client and the confused and chaotic state she was in danger of feeling, should she surrender to what therapy was offering her. My colleague's empathic stance and positive regard for me enabled me to see that even though my responses had not been optimal, they were the understandable consequence of strong transference forces together with the triggering of my own wounds around racism, exclusion, bigotry, and prejudice—which I had previously thought resolved, but which were still influential. Furthermore, I was reminded of the inevitable presence of prejudice, rigidity and bigotry, often so subtle in their transformation. Kahn quotes Donna Orange as saying, "We must know and acknowledge our countertransference, our co-transference, our point of view or perspective, if we are to be capable of empathy […]. We must acknowledge the lenses through which we are reading the text in order to do authentic psychoanalytic work." (Kahn, 1996, p. 35) I began to see that this rupture, this fallibility, this lack of understanding, this empathic impasse might also be an opportunity for repair and growth. It was clear that if there was such a possibility, this could only happen through transparency, appropriate honesty, and empathy, and not through a protective/defensive and manipulative use of countertransferential responses.

The exchange that ensued in the next session was so simple and yet so profoundly transformative.

She came in. Stormy and sullen. She sat down. I remained quiet and so did she.

I said (T1): "You seem angry and resigned."
    S1: "What's the point …"
    T2: Silence …
    S2: Silence …
    T3: "You didn't get the answer you deserved from me at the end of the last session … it seemed really unfair …"
    S3: "Yes. Very unfair! I thought of ending …"

T4:   Silence.

S4:   "I felt I deserved to know that … it was so … so … disrespectful! Here I am, letting you in … I've never done that with anyone before. Do you think that's easy?"

T5:   "It has been really hard …"

S5:   "Very …" (She starts crying) … "It feels like I am truly alone … "I am really alone, like always …" (she is sobbing).

T6:   "Oh Sara …"

She continued crying for a considerable amount of time and then:

S6:   "I have to tell you something … no one knows …"

Sara went on to say that when she was five years' old she walked into her mother's room in the middle of the night because she was having a nightmare. She realised that her uncle was sleeping in her mother's bed with her mother. They did not see her.

She went on to become the silent, feverish observer of an affair which she thought continued for a number of years.

After this disclosure, issues around identity receded into the background. It was clear in this case, how identity trauma had been used as a defence, to mask the primary traumas of neglect, danger, betrayal, and the breaking of codes lurking within the family rather than outside it. In our "co-transference" (Kahn, 1996), Sara played out the dynamic of betrayal and isolation and I responded with betrayal, partisanship and failing empathy. This state of play was reversed in this short exchange by creating conditions of true safety anew, by acknowledging my failure, and allowing Sara to fill the intersubjective space with her full self, as I suspended mine momentarily. Sara was moved to express her hidden trauma, which she usually disconnected from, as an important factor in her unhappiness. In the coming months we were able to move on to exploring and understanding, through active empathic inquiry in Stolorow's terms.

But what was it in those six interchanges between us which fostered such movement?

When Sara came into the room on the day that this transcribed exchange took place, it was evident that we were both vividly engaged with the previous session, as if it had only happened the day before.

Our impasse had alarmed us both, and the possibility of our sessions ending had emerged in my mind too.

She appeared stormy and resigned and it felt important to ver-balise what I was seeing and experiencing (T1). The sense of futility that this reflection identified, struck a chord (S1), "What's the point", fell into the space, like a drop into a pool of still pointlessness. There was nothing to say to that (T2), but merely to sit and be immersed in it. What was pointless in that moment was our process and the fact that, at her ultimate test, I could not be trusted. I had secrets I could not reveal. Like her mother. Furthermore, I had rejected the aspects of herself which were not for growth and sided with the ones I considered valuable; I was proposing conditions to her worthiness. Mearns says, "If we are to relate fully to our client in his growth proc-ess we need to attend to *all* aspects of his experience—the voices that push for movement and also those which urge caution, because they are both parts of the growth process" (Mearns, 2003, p. 19). In that moment the unfair and rejecting quality of my defensive response to her question in our previous session featured strongly in my mind. I expressed this (T3). She vigorously agreed, and my indication that I was on her side in that painful rejection, allowed her to say what she might have otherwise not said—that she wished to end (S3). Again, the space demanded to be left unfilled (T4). She became bolder in expressing her indignation at my response and her right to have a more honest answer in a relationship that purports to search for truth. She also spoke of her despair that this relationship she had begun to engage in, despite her strong reservations, confirmed all she had feared and all she had experienced during her life—abandonment, lack of loyalty, respect, transparency, power, and recognition. Letting her know that I could feel how hard it felt (T5), gave her permission to experience her pain as legitimate. Genuinely accepting and validating her rage made space for the feelings of utter loneliness which plagued her whole life (S5). I could feel how heartbroken she was (T6). That deep companionship between us allowed her to tell me where her real heartbreak lay (S6).

I think that what is important in this tiny exchange, is that it illus-trates how the position of the therapist *next* to the client, not ahead nor behind, following her leading cues in what she was expressing, allows for such deep validation, that the client is able to explore areas which appear frightening and dangerous. We were just "being" together, not thinking. It is, as Shlien said: "the exquisite awareness of dual experience that restores consciousness of self" (Shlien, 1971, p. 164). I would add, for both.

Conclusion

In this paper I have tried to show the importance of empathy as an essential element in deep communication processes with the client. Empathy contributes to the creation of a secure context, in which previously traumatic and disavowed material may emerge and be explored. I have used Carl Rogers' thinking to articulate my understanding of empathy and the ways in which I have seen it being effective in the consulting room. Carl Rogers has described the process in clinical, experiential terms and through this has captured the verbal and non-verbal conditions involved in such communication. I have also argued that a more active approach is crucial to development, and in my view fine attunement and empathy does include, when appropriate, the tentative proposal of interpretations of unconscious and conscious material. From an intersubjective perspective, failures, such as the one described, are opportunities. It was through a failure in empathy that we were able to make an important breakthrough, but it was through the return to empathic communication that we were able to make meaningful contact and progress.

References

Baron-Cohen, S. (2011). *Zero Degrees Empathy: A New Theory of Human Cruelty*. London: Allen Lane.

Ellis, A., & Abrams, M. (2009). *Personality Theories: Critical Perspectives*. London: Sage.

Ferenczi, S. (1928). The elasticity of psychoanalytic technique. In: M. Balint (Ed.), *Final Contributions to the Problems and Methods of Psychoanalysis, Vol. 3* (pp. 87–102). New York: Basic Books, 1955. [as cited in Rachman, 1988]

Freud, S. (1905c). *Jokes and their Relation to the Unconscious. S. E., 8*. London: Hogarth. [as cited in Pigman, 1995]

Freud, S. (1912e). Recommendations to physicians practising psychoanalysis. *S. E., 12*. London: Hogarth. [as cited in Pigman, 1995]

Kahn, E. (1996). The Intersubjective perspective and the client-centred approach: Are they one at the core? *Psychotherapy, 33*: 30–42.

Kahn, E., & Rachman, A. W. (2000). Carl Rogers and Heinz Kohut: A historical perspective. *Psychoanalytic Psychology, 17*: 294–312.

Kohut, H. (1959). Introspection, empathy and psychoanalysis—an examination of the relationship between mode of observation and theory. *Journal of the American Psychoanalytic Association, 7*: 459–483.

Kohut, H. (1984). *How Does Analysis Cure?* Chicago: University of Chicago Press.

Lotze, H. (1858). *Mikrokosmos. Ideen zur Natur-geschichte und Geschichte der Menschleit. Versuch einer Anthropologie, Bd.2*, ed. R. Schmidt. Leipzig: Mainer, 1923, 6th edition. [as cited in Pigman, 1995]

Mearns, D. (2003). *Developing Person-Centred Counselling.* London: Sage.

Mearns, D., & Thorne, B. (1988). *Person-Centred Counseling in Action.* London: Sage.

Mollon, P. (2003). *Releasing the Self: The Healing Legacy of Heinz Kohut.* London: Whurr.

Pigman, G. W. (1995). Freud and the history of empathy. *International Journal of Psycho-Analysis, 76*: 237–256.

Rachman, A. W. (1988). The rule of empathy: Sandor Ferenczi's pioneering contributions to the empathic method in psychoanalysis. *The Journal of the American Academy of Psychoanalysis and Dynamic Psychiatry, 16*: 1–27.

Rogers, C. R. (1951). *Client-Centred Therapy.* London: Constable.

Rogers, C. R. (1957). The necessary and sufficient conditions for personality change. *Journal of Consulting Psychology, 21*: 95–103.

Rogers, C. R. (1980). *A Way of Being.* Boston: Houghton Mifflin

Rogers, C. R. (1986). Client-centred/Person-centred approach to therapy. In: H. Kirschenbaum, & V. Land Henderson (Eds.), *The Carl Rogers Reader* (pp. 135–152). London: Constable, 1990.

Schore, A. N. (1994). *Affect Regulation and the Origin of the Self: The Neurobiology of Emotional Development.* Hillsdale, NJ: Lawrence Erlbaum.

Sharma, R. M. (1992). Empathy—A retrospective on its development in psychotherapy. *Australian and New Zealand Journal of Psychiatry, 26*: 377–390.

Shlien, J. M. (1971). A client-centred approach to schizophrenia: First approximation. In: C. R. Rogers & B. Stevens (Eds.), *Person to Person* (pp. 149–165). New York: Pocket Books.

Stolorow, R. D., & Atwood, G. E. (1992). The realms of the unconscious. In: S. A. Mitchell, & L. Aron (Eds.), *Relational Psychoanalysis: The Emergence of a Tradition* (pp. 367–378). Hillsdale NJ: The Analytic Press, 1999.

Stuber, K. (2013). Empathy. In: E. N. Zalta (Ed.), *The Stanford Encyclopedia of Philosophy (Summer 2013 Edition).* Available at: http://plato.stanford.edu/archives/sum2013/entries/empathy/. Accessed August 24, 2013.

Reading list

Alvarez, A. (1992). *Live Company*. London: Routledge.

Begley, S. (2009). *The Plastic Mind*. London: Constable.

Blackmore, S. (2006). *Conversations on Consciousness*. Oxford: Oxford University Press.

Bloom, S. L. (1997). *Creating Sanctuary: Toward the Evolution of Sane Societies*. New York: Routledge.

Bloom, S. L. (Ed.) (2001). *Violence: A Public Health Epidemic and a Public Health Approach*. London: Karnac.

Bloom, S. L. (2010). The mental health aspects of IPV: Survivors, professionals, and systems. In: A. P. Giardino, & E. R. Giardino (Eds.), *Intimate Partner Violence, Domestic Violence, and Spousal Abuse: A Resource for Professionals Working With Children and Families* (pp. 207–250). St. Louis, MO: STM Learning.

Bloom, S. L. (2010). Trauma-organized systems and parallel process. In: N. Tehrani (Ed.), *Managing Trauma in the Workplace—Supporting Workers and the Organization* (pp. 139–153). London: Routledge.

Bloom, S. L., & Farragher, B. (2010). *Destroying Sanctuary: The Crisis in Human Service Delivery Systems*. Oxford: Oxford University Press.

Bloom, S. L., & Reichert, M. (1998). *Bearing Witness: Violence and Collective Responsibility*. Binghampton, NY: Haworth Press.

Bloom, S. L., & Vargas, L. (Eds.) (2007). *Loss, Hurt and Hope: The Complex Issues of Bereavement, Trauma and Children*. Newcastle: Cambridge Scholars Publishing.

Buber, M. (1970). *I and Thou*. New York: Charles Scribners & Sons.

Cooper, P. (2010). *The Zen Impulse and the Psychoanalytic Encounter*. New York: Routledge.

Fosha, D. (2000). *The Transforming Power Of Affect*. New York: Basic Books.

Gerhardt, S. (2004). *Why Love Matters: How Affection Shapes a Baby's Brain*. London: Brunner Routledge.

Gerhardt, S. (2011). *The Selfish Society: How We All Forgot to Love One Another and Made Money Instead*. London: Simon & Schuster.

Gilbert, P. (2005). *Compassion: Conceptualisations, Research and Use in Psychotherapy*. London: Routledge.

Gordon, P. (2009). *The Hope of Therapy*. Ross-on-Wye: PCCS Books.

Hopkins, L. (2006). *False Self: The Life of Masud Khan*. New York: Other Press.

James, O. (2007). *They F*** You Up: How to Survive Family Life*. London: Bloomsbury.

James, O. (2010). *How Not to F*** Them Up*. London: Vermilion.

Kirschenbaum, H., & Land Henderson, V. (Eds.) (1990). *The Carl Rogers Reader*. London: Constable.

Knoblauch, S. (2000). *The Musical Edge of Therapeutic Dialogue*. Hillsdale, NJ: Analytic Press.

Knox, J. (2011). *Self-Agency in Psychotherapy: Attachment, Autonomy and Intimacy*. London: Norton.

Malloch, S., & Trevarthen, C. (Eds.) (2009). *Communicative Musicality*. Oxford: Oxford University Press.

Maroda, K. (1999). *Seduction, Surrender and Transformation*. Hillsdale, NJ: Analytic Press.

Mitchell, S. (2000). *Relationality: From Attachment to Intersubjectivity*. Hillsdale, NJ: Analytic Press.

Proust, M. (2003). *In Search of Lost Time Vol. 1: The Way by Swann's*. London: Penguin.

Rilke, R. M. (1993). *Letters to a Young Poet*. London: Norton.

Rilke, R. M. (2011). *Selected Poems: With Parallel German Text*. Oxford: Oxford University Press.

Shakespeare, William: *King Lear*. Arden Shakespeare Complete Works. London: Bloomsbury.

Sroufe, A., Egeland, B., Carlson, E., & Collins, A. (2005). *The Development of the Person: The Minnesota Study of Risk and Adaptation from Birth to Adulthood*. New York: Guilford Press.

Wallin, D. J. (2007). *Attachment in Psychotherapy*. New York: Guilford Press.

The Bowlby Centre

Promoting attachment and inclusion

Since 1976 The Bowlby Centre (formerly known as CAPP) has developed as an organisation committed to the practice of attachment-based psychoanalytic psychotherapy. The Bowlby Centre is a dynamic, rapidly developing charity which aims both to train attachment-based psychoanalytic psychotherapists and to deliver a psychotherapy service to those who are most marginalised and frequently excluded from long term psychotherapy.

We provide a four year part time psychotherapy training accredited by the UKCP and operate a psychotherapy referral service for the public including the low cost Blues Project. The Bowlby Centre has a wealth of experience in the fields of attachment and loss and particular expertise in working with trauma and abuse. As part of our ongoing commitment to anti-discriminatory practice we offer a consultation service to the public and private sectors and are engaged in outreach and special projects working with care leavers, women experiencing violence and abuse, offenders and ex offenders, people struggling with addiction to drugs, alcohol, eating difficulties or self harm, and to individuals and groups in a wide variety of mental health settings.

We run short courses on "Attachment and dissociation", and "The application of attachment theory to clinical issues" including learning disabilities. The Bowlby Centre organises conferences including the annual John Bowlby memorial lecture, and has a series of publications which aim to further thinking and development in the field of attachment.

Bowlby Centre members participate extensively in all aspects of the field, making outstanding theoretical, research, and clinical contributions. Their cutting edge work is consistently published in the leading journals and monographs.

The Bowlby Centre values:

- The Centre believes that mental distress has its origin in failed and inadequate attachment relationships in early life and is best treated in the context of a long-term human relationship.
- Attachment relationships are shaped in the real world and impacted upon by poverty, discrimination, and social inequality. The impact of the social world will be part of the therapy.
- Psychotherapy should be available to all, and from an attachment-based psychoanalytic perspective, especially those discriminated against or described as "unsuitable" for therapy.
- Psychotherapy should be provided with respect, warmth, openness, a readiness to interact and relate, and free from discrimination of any kind.
- Those who have been silenced about their experiences and survival strategies must have their reality acknowledged and not pathologised.
- The Bowlby Centre values inclusiveness, access, diversity, authenticity, and excellence. All participants in our organisation share the responsibility for anti-discriminatory practice in relation to race, ethnicity, gender, sexuality, age, (dis)ability, religion, class, educational, and learning style.

Patrons

Sir Richard Bowlby
Dr Elaine Arnold

Trustees

Jeremy Rutter—Chair
Janie Harvey-Douglas
Prue Norton

For more information please contact:

The Bowlby Centre
1 Highbury Crescent
London
N5 1RN
Phone: 020 7700 5070
Email: admin@thebowlbycentre.org.uk
Web: www.thebowlbycentre.org.uk

INDEX

Indexer: Dr Laurence Errington